DAVID M. SHOUP

A Warrior against War

HOWARD JABLON

ROWMAN & LITTLEFIELD PUBLISHERS, INC.
Lanham • Boulder • New York • Toronto • Oxford

ROWMAN & LITTLEFIELD PUBLISHERS, INC.

Published in the United States of America
by Rowman & Littlefield Publishers, Inc.
A wholly owned subsidary of The Rowman & Littlefield Publishing
Group, Inc.
4501 Forbes Boulevard, Suite 200, Lanham, Maryland 20706
www.rowmanlittlefield.com

PO Box 317
Oxford
OX2 9RU, UK

British Library Cataloguing in Publication Information Available

Library of Congress Cataloging-in-Publication Data

Jablon, Howard.
    David M. Shoup : a warrior against war / Howard Jablon.
        p. cm. — (Biographies in American foreign policy)
    Includes bibliographical references and index.
    ISBN 0-7425-4487-7 (alk. paper)
    1. Shoup, David M. (David Monroe), 1904– 2. Generals—United
States—Biography. 3. United States. Marine Corps—Biography.
I. Title. II. Series.

    E840.5.S47J33 2005
    359.9'6'092—dc22   2004026082

Printed in the United States of America

∞™ The paper used in this publication meets the minimum
requirements of American National Standard for Information
Sciences—Permanence of Paper for Printed Library Materials,
ANSI/NISO Z39.48-1992.

In loving memory of my parents Harris and Pauline Jablon

Official portrait of David M. Shoup, 22nd Commandant of the Marine Corps. *Source:* Marine Corps University Research Archives.

Contents

Acknowledgments

I am indebted to many people who made the completion of this biography possible. At the outset, Brigadier General Edwin H. Simmons and his staff at the Marine Corps History and Museums Division provided encouragement and guidance. Later on, Patricia Mullen and the staff at Marine Corps University provided vital archival material. Equally helpful were the archivists at the Hoover Institution on War, Peace, and Revolution at Stanford University, and the archivists at the John Fitzgerald Kennedy Library. Our research librarian at Purdue University North Central, Alicia Maehler, provided necessary assistance as well.

Those who suffered through the reading of early drafts of the manuscript deserve special praise. Allan R. Millett and Joseph H. Alexander corrected many errors in fact and judgment. The series editor, Joseph A. Fry, made my work more intelligent and intelligible. My secretary and typist, Terry Blaschke, and my copyeditors, Georgiana Strickland, Beth Rudnick, and Connie Szawara, created order where none existed.

I appreciate the material support I received from Purdue University North Central that granted me sabbatical leave on two occasions to work on this project. And I appreciate the emotional support I received from my wife, Rita.

Chronology

1904

November 8	Theodore Roosevelt is elected, defeating Alton B. Parker, Democrat; Eugene V. Debs, Socialist; and Thomas E. Watson, Populist.
December 6	Roosevelt Corollary to the Monroe Doctrine transforms it from nonintervention to intervention in the Western Hemisphere.
December 30	David M. Shoup is born in Ash Grove, near Battle Ground, Indiana.

1905

July 29	Taft-Katsura Memorandum: United States gives Japan a free hand in Korea; Japan disclaims designs on Philippines.
August 9	Portsmouth Conference: Theodore Roosevelt mediates ending of Russo-Japanese war.

1906

February 24	Gentleman's Agreement: Japan makes voluntary restrictions on emigration of Japanese laborers intending to work in the United States.
June 29	Theodore Roosevelt signs a bill authorizing building of the Panama Canal.
October 11	San Francisco school board imposes segregation on Japanese school children. Roosevelt intervenes and secures its rescindment.

1908

November 30	Root-Takahira Agreement provides for maintaining the status quo in the Pacific, reaffirms Open Door in China. Japan interprets agreement as recognizing their

dominance in Korea and southern Manchuria.

1909

July 15   Taft displays his "dollar diplomacy" by appealing to the Chinese regent to allow U.S. participation in consortium to finance railroad construction.

1911

June 6   Knox-Castrillo Convention grants the United States the right of intervention in Nicaragua to take over their custom house to secure payment of debts.

August 14   Marines land in response to civil war in Nicaragua to protect American interests, remain until 1933.

1912

August 2   Lodge Corollary: Senator Henry Cabot Lodge introduces resolution declaring concern over a corporation possessing an area of strategic importance to the United States, prompted by a Japanese syndicate's attempt to purchase land in lower California. Extends Monroe Doctrine to non-European powers and to companies. Shoup's brother warns him that war with Japan is inevitable.

1914

April 21   U.S. forces bombard Vera Cruz and occupy the city in response to alleged affronts to the American flag and to prevent war supplies from reaching the city. United States and Mexico close to war.

1915

May 7   Sinking of the *Lusitania* by German U-boat results in loss of American lives. Wilson sends a series of protest notes, the last representing an ultimatum.

July 29   Wilson orders marines to Haiti. They land on the 29th and impose military occupation in response to civil war there. Haiti becomes a U.S. protectorate.

1916

March 15	Pursuit of Pancho Villa in Mexico by General John J. Pershing, ordered in response to Villa's raids into American territory. Ill will between Mexico and the United States mounts on the eve of U.S. entry into World War I.
November 29	Full military occupation of Santo Domingo. U.S. naval officers in charge of internal administration until 1924.

1917

April 16	United States declares war on Germany.
November 2	In Lansing-Ishii agreement, United States recognizes that Japan has special interests in China.

1918

November 11	Armistice brings World War I to a close.

1919

November 18	Wilson urges rejection of Senator Lodge's resolution, which effectively rejects ratification of the Versailles Treaty.

1921

June	Shoup graduates from Covington High School.

1921–1922

November 12–February 6	Washington Armament Conference, convened by the United States, results in nine treaties. Among the major agreements are a five-power treaty erecting a naval construction holiday and establishing a ratio of capital ships; a four-power treaty that ends the Anglo-Japanese alliances; and a nine-power treaty reaffirming the Open Door policy.

1924

	The United States signs a new treaty with the Dominican Republic that ends Dominican occupation; U.S. Marines are withdrawn.

1926

June	Shoup graduates from DePauw University.
June 26	Shoup enlists in the Marines.

August	Shoup serves briefly in the Army Reserve.
August–September	Shoup is a student at the Marine Basic School in Philadelphia.

1926–1927

October–February	Shoup is on the football squad.

1927

March 24	Nanking Incident, in which communists attack foreigners, prompts an international force to intervene to protect Shanghai.
April–December	Shoup serves with China Expeditionary Force.

1928

February–July	Shoup returns to Basic School in Philadelphia.
July	Shoup completes Basic School.
October	Shoup is a student naval aviator at Pensacola until May 1929; does not complete the courses.

1929

	Shoup is a student at Sea School.
May	Shoup is a naval air station student; does not complete program.

1929–1931

	Shoup is assigned to Marine detachment's five-inch battery and serves on the USS Maryland.
	Shoup marries Zola DeHaven.

1931

September	Mukden incident in Manchuria, in which Japanese use railroad explosion as an excuse to seize the arsenal and launch a campaign ending in the seizure of three eastern provinces.

1932

January 7	Secretary of State Stimson announces the nonrecognition doctrine: the United States will not recognize any territorial gains through force in China.
	Shoup is promoted to first lieutenant.

| | Shoup is at Marine base in San Diego (company officer headquarters). |
| September | Japanese establish a protectorate over Manchikuo (Manchuria). |

1932–1933

| | Shoup is an athletic officer at Bremerton, Washington, naval yard. |

1933

| February | League of Nations adopts Stimson's nonrecognition doctrines. |

1933–1934

| April | Shoup is at the Civilian Conservation Corps camp in Boville, Idaho. |
| June–May | Shoup is assigned to temporary duty with the Civilian Conservation Corps. |

1934

April	Japan proclaims Amau Doctrine.
May	Saito's Eight-Point Memorandum.
	Shoup returns to Bremerton, Washington.
	Shoup is in Seattle as a pistol and rifle instructor.
December	Shoup arrives in China.

1934–1936

| December–May | Shoup is assigned to American legation, Peking, China. Is on artillery and rifle team; in charge of winning pistol team; athletics and sports officer, post pistol team. |

1936

| | Shoup is promoted to captain. |

1937

	Shoup is a competitor in Western Division rifle and pistol competition.
	Shoup is a student in the junior course, Quantico, Virginia.
July	Japanese and Chinese troops clash near Peking, leads to large-scale encounters in northern China, marking the beginning of Sino-Japanese war.
October	Roosevelt's "quarantine aggressors" speech in Chicago, apparently a reference to Japan.

	December	In Panay incident; Japanese bombers attack an American ship. Japanese apologize.

1937–1940

Shoup remains at Quantico, Virginia, as instructor.

1938

| | September | Munich Conference to resolve German occupation of Czechoslovakia ends by appeasing Hitler with the Sudetenland. |

1939

| | September | Germany invades Poland, starting World War II. |
| | November | U.S. Neutrality Act repeals the arms embargo and permits export of arms and belligerents on a cash-and-carry basis. |

1940

Shoup is at Headquarters and Service Company, Fleet Marine Force, San Diego, California.

1941

| | April | Shoup is promoted to major. |

1941–1942

| | July–February | Shoup is assigned to a First Marine Brigade (Provisional) in Iceland. |

1941

| | December 7 | Japanese bomb Pearl Harbor. |

1942

| | April–July | Shoup serves at San Diego Recruit Depot and is assistant division G3. |
| | August | Shoup is promoted to lieutenant colonel. |

1942–1944

| | August–October | Shoup goes to New Zealand with the Fleet Marine Force, Second Marine Division. He is an observer at Guadalcanal, assigned at division G3, until November 1943. |

1943

| | June | Shoup is wounded at Rendova. |
| | November | Shoup is commanding officer of the assault forces at Tarawa and is appointed colonel. |

1944

July   Shoup participates in Saipan and Tinian
                    assaults.

1945

August 6   Bombing of Hiroshima.
August 9   Bombing of Nagasaki.
August 10   Japanese surrender ends World War II in the
                    Pacific.

1946

January–   Shoup serves as assistant chief of staff,
   September   Division of Plans and Policies. He is also a
                    member of the board that recommends reor-
                    ganization and consolidation of Quarter-
                    master and Paymaster Departments into a
                    single Supply Department.

1953

April   Shoup is designated assistant fiscal director
                    and promoted to brigadier general.

1953–1956

July 1953–   Shoup is named fiscal director.
   May 1956

1955

March–   Shoup serves on Standing Committee for
   August   Continuing Review, Appropriation,
                    Accounting and Data Processing.
September   Shoup is promoted to major general while
                    serving as fiscal director.

1956

April–May   Shoup is named inspector general of Recruit
                    Training. Six recruits drown in Ribbon
                    Creek incident.

1958

                    Shoup is designated commanding officer of
                    Third Marine Division, Okinawa.

1959

January   Castro comes to power in Cuba.
November 2   While commanding general of Parris Island
                    Depot, Shoup is promoted to lieutenant
                    general.

1960

January	Shoup is nominated by President Dwight Eisenhower to be twenty-second commandant of the Marine Corps. After Senate confirmation, he assumes his duties and is promoted to general.
November	John F. Kennedy is elected president. War in Vietnam.
December	National Liberation Front is established in Vietnam.

1961

January 17	Eisenhower warns about the growing threat of a military-industrial complex.
	Bay of Pigs invasion fails.
	Berlin Wall is set up.

1962

October	Cuban missile crisis.

1963

	Nuclear test ban treaty is signed.
November 1	President Diem is overthrown in Vietnam.
November 22	President Kennedy is assassinated. Lyndon Johnson becomes president.
December	Shoup's tour as commandant ends.

1964

February	North Vietnam is bombed by the United States for the first time (Operation Flaming Dart).
August 7	Gulf of Tonkin Resolution is passed.

1965

March 8	American combat troops are sent to Vietnam. War protests start on university campuses.

1966

May 14	Hearing on Vietnam conducted by Senate Foreign Relations Committee. Shoup's "blood soaked fingers" speech.

1967

	Antiwar protests increase. Protesters march on Pentagon. American troops in Vietnam number 540,000.

1968

Shoup testifies before Senate Foreign Relations Committee.
Antiwar Mobilization Day.

1969

April Shoup and Donovan publish "The New American Militarism" in *Atlantic Monthly*. Vietnam "moratorium" held by war protesters. Bombing of Cambodia. Withdrawal of American troops from Vietnam.

October 15, November 15 Antiwar demonstrations held in Washington, D.C.

1970

May 4 Colonel James A. Donovan's book *Militarism USA* contains foreword by Shoup. War protests increase. Students killed at Kent State University.

1971

June 13 Pentagon Papers are published.

1972

April 15 United States mines Haiphong harbor in North Vietnam, and Nixon orders Christmas bombing of North Vietnam.

1973

January 27 United States withdraws from Vietnam as Paris agreement leads to cease-fire.

1974

August 9 Nixon resigns.

1975

April 30 South Vietnam falls. North Vietnamese take Saigon.

1983

January 13 General Shoup dies at age seventy-eight.

Introduction:
Task Force Tarawa

Marine Corps units in Iraq today are designated Task Force Tarawa, commemorating one of the fiercest battles in the Pacific during World War II. The battle of Tarawa, actually an assault on Betio island in the Tarawa atoll, was a savagely fought engagement leaving only 146 Japanese defenders alive and more than 3,000 Americans dead or wounded. Earlier battles, such as Guadalcanal, claimed as many American casualties, but the losses at Tarawa took place in just seventy-six hours, not the six months required to take Guadalcanal; additionally, the ratio of killed to wounded was higher at Tarawa. When news of the bloody victory at Tarawa reached the United States, the public reacted as though it were a terrible defeat. Immediately, a storm of controversy raged over "bloody Tarawa," thereby prompting President Franklin D. Roosevelt to conduct an intensive public relations campaign to soothe an aroused electorate. Roosevelt succeeded in assuaging the public's ire, but the debate over Tarawa continued years after the war ended. General Holland M. Smith, one of the commanding generals at Tarawa, later wrote that he believed that the battle was a tragic mistake.[1]

Among the heroes of that controversial battle was David M. Shoup, who helped plan the attack, who rallied his troops during the critical first day and a half of battle, and who was the only surviving Medal of Honor recipient. But it was not the last time that Shoup would find himself in a controversial struggle. After Shoup retired from the Marine Corps, he joined the Vietnam War protest movement in 1966. Like other protesting senior officers, he attacked American involvement there as a senseless intrusion in a civil war unrelated to national security. His position was not new. It was a continuation of his strong aversion to sending troops to the Vietnam quagmire when he was commandant of the Marine Corps. When an aide suggested sending Marines to Vietnam, Shoup retorted that it was like "pissin' down a rat hole." As a war protestor, Shoup repeated that message in milder language in public meetings, congressional hearings, and publications.

Shoup was more than a war hero and protestor. He was an officer whose career culminated in his appointment as commandant of the Marine Corps by President Dwight D. Eisenhower in 1959, a post he held until 1963. When John F. Kennedy succeeded Eisenhower, Shoup became a supporting actor in the dramatic events of the Kennedy administration. Like the other Joint Chiefs of Staff, initially he was on the fringe of decision making. That soon changed as Kennedy recognized the value of the blunt, sometimes vulgar Marine general. Shoup rapidly emerged as the president's favorite Chief. When Shoup's tour as commandant was ending, Kennedy asked Shoup to continue. Shoup declined, but Kennedy persisted in making overtures to him to serve the administration in some other capacity.

During his tour as commandant under Eisenhower, Shoup's contributions to the formulation of foreign policy were nonexistent. Most of his time was spent on improving the morale and combat readiness of the Corps. Opportunities to guide national security decisions came later when Kennedy sought his advice on the nuclear test ban treaty, Laos, and Vietnam. Usually, records were not kept of Kennedy's conversations with Shoup. There is, however, sufficient direct and indirect evidence to conclude that Shoup played a role in the development of foreign policy.

Apart from his place in the Eisenhower and Kennedy administrations, Shoup's life illustrated the first three-quarters of U.S. history, whether in war or in times of peace. Born during the Progressive Era, he absorbed the idealism and antipathies of that period. Throughout his adult life he referred to himself as an "Indiana plowboy," a disingenuous reference to himself as a simple rube but one who could not be fooled by slick manipulators. As he matured, he retained the progressive suspicion of economic power and imperialism. Later, when he was a young officer serving two tours of duty in China, he reflected on the economic exploitation of that country and the unwanted American interference in its political life. While in China he also learned to respect Asian soldiers when he witnessed the highly disciplined behavior of Japanese troops. Subsequently, during World War II, he was to learn firsthand just how effectively they could fight.

Shoup never intended to be a soldier. He stumbled into a military career as he tried desperately to ease his dire financial circumstances. Once in the Marine Corps, however, he learned to love it. He became an old-fashioned, hard-boiled marine whose exacting standards and harsh discipline instilled fear in his subordinates. Only his sharp wit softened his leadership. Throughout his career, and notably when he was commandant of the Marine Corps, he placed his trust in well-trained men, not machines, though he understood the value of technology and was, at times, innovative. He disdained the elitist affectations of some fellow officers, often showing more respect for enlisted men and noncommissioned officers than those with high rank. Always the hardheaded pragmatist, he had no patience with politicking inside or outside the Corps. He discouraged junior officers who tried to form alliances to further their careers, and he resisted as best he could the meddling of outside agencies, like the CIA, in Corps matters. Shoup had a sharp analytical way of looking at military matters. His mathematical mind was always evident in his decision making, even his poker playing. Consequently, he ridiculed mindless conformity and wishful thinking in the Corps. On one occasion, during the Cuban missile crisis, he deprecated the amateurish judgment of fellow senior officers who underestimated the price of victory.

Above all, Shoup's war protesting during the Vietnam conflict was the defining moment of his life. It brought together in a climactic way a lifetime of experiences: a long-held suspicion of business pressure on government and a distaste for foreign misadventures, a solid judgment that interference in nationalist uprisings was futile and an inappropriate use of the military, a tenacious courage of conviction equal to his valor in battle, and an enduring love of country and Corps.

Shoup is a fascinating subject in his own right. He is a study in contradictions. One aspect of his personality was the tough, hard-boiled, no-nonsense Marine Corps officer; another aspect of his personality was his sensitivity, which he often expressed in poetry. Some subordinates, particularly senior officers, found him cruel; junior and noncommissioned officers found him supportive. No one with any sense challenged him at poker. And everyone respected him for his intelligence, hard work, and devotion to the Corps.

Humor was also a part of Shoup's multifaceted personality. He always managed to see the lighter side of life, even under the dreariest of circumstances. On one occasion, when he was resting from the

Figure I.1.   Colonel Shoup, chief of staff Second Marine Division, reads *How to Win Friends and Influence People* on Saipan Island, July 1944. *Source:* Marine Corps University Research Archives.

fatigue of battle on Saipan during World War II, he found time to pose for a photograph. He sat on a large tin can with a dead Japanese soldier at his feet pretending to read Dale Carnegie's *How to Win Friends and Influence People*. It was typical of Shoup's way of relieving the stress of battle.

If Shoup were alive now, he would appreciate how some marines use humor to cope with the discomforts of war. Just before the outbreak of hostilities in Iraq, at the end of March 2003, a *New York Times* reporter noted how one marine in Task Force Tarawa coped with the boredom of camp life. First Lieutenant Josh Cusworth, a battalion intelligence officer, admitted, "I don't take anything seriously."[2] Even in the middle of burning trash, the young lieutenant could quip that now he could tell his friends back home that "literally, we lived in a dump."[3]

But war was no laughing matter to Shoup. He always carried the memory of fallen comrades at Tarawa, reliving that battle at reunions with survivors. The searing experience of combat and the terrible price of victory at Tarawa explain why he protested what he deemed the shameful waste of life in Vietnam.

Notes

1. Holland M. Smith and Percy Finch, *Coral and Brass* (New York, 1949), 134.
2. *New York Times*, April 2, 2003, B6.
3. *New York Times*, April 2, 2003, B6.

1

Hoosier Plowboy

On November 13, 1960, David M. Shoup returned home to Indiana to be honored on Dave Shoup Day. It was a Veterans Day celebration to pay tribute to the local hero. He spoke to the crowd about growing up in Covington and how he met his wife, Zola, at a party there in 1917. Though convinced at first sight that this young girl would be his wife, it was fifteen years before he married her. But he acknowledged, "Without this little lady there would have been no more me." It was a tribute to an enduring connection to his past. For the present, he cautioned his audience, "Of one thing I am certain. Soon we must learn to live together on this earth or we shall die together." He wondered "whether mankind has put its best talent to the important task of eliminating war."[1] On other occasions he reiterated this tribute to his origins and warning to the hometown folks. A year later, on August 18, 1961, Shoup returned to Indiana for the sesquicentennial of the Battle of Tippecanoe. At Battle Ground, Indiana, near his birthplace, he reminded his audience of the lesson of that battle: "Neither wealth nor complex machines can ever be substituted for our fighting men," a message he often sent to his superiors. And later that day he recalled a comment made to him by his brother in 1912 when they were living near that battle site. His older brother had told him, "We some day will have to fight the Japanese."[2] Shoup survived the war his brother had predicted, a grim reminder that Indiana was connected to a larger and often hostile world.

Throughout his adult life, David Shoup referred to himself as an Indiana plowboy. Often he used the reference to his origins to berate someone he thought was trying to deceive him or who had acted foolishly. The label was appropriate since he never forgot where he was born

and the stark realities of being raised in rural poverty. The circumstances of his birth near Battle Ground on December 30, 1904, may
seem prophetic for a man who became a war hero and general, but
most of his childhood was spent on a farm near Covington, Indiana,
a small city on the banks of the Wabash. In many ways the city re-
tains the atmosphere Shoup knew when he lived there. As in other
communities in the state, residents remain loyal, sometimes fiercely
devoted, to their hometown. There and elsewhere, Hoosier hysteria
is more than a passion for basketball. Every year the statewide basketball tournament becomes a manifestation of provincial patriot-
ism. At heart, Shoup shared those strong communal attachments.
He was always proud to be a Hoosier.

People in Indiana refer to themselves as "Hoosiers," but no one
knows how this word originated. And while its meaning is subject to
various interpretations, the inhabitants of the state see themselves as
unique, or at least different from other regional stereotypes. In the
nineteenth century the term often had a negative connotation, which
persisted into the twentieth century. Meredith Nicholson, in 1904,
lamented "the assumption in Eastern quarters that [the Hoosier] is a
wild man of the woods."[3] During the 1920s, when the Ku Klux Klan
dominated the state, outside Indiana, Hoosiers appeared to be
provincial bigots.

Within the state, many of the characteristics outsiders ridiculed
were embraced as virtues. As the twentieth century unfolded,
Hoosiers glorified their image as rubes and contrasted it with the sor-
did life of urban industrial America. Paradoxically, their perspective
persisted even as more and more Hoosiers moved to the cities. They
idealized their earlier simpler life in the state song, "On the Banks of
the Wabash Far Away," and the state poem, "God crowned her hill
with beauty." Above all, they believed they had something special,
something enduring and worth preserving. As the state song and
poem suggest, Hoosiers clung to their traditional agrarian values.
They were proudly and profoundly conservative.

Cultural life in Indiana romanticized rural small-town values at
the turn of the century. In popular writing, for example, the state's authors produced such a large number of best-selling books that it became a golden age of Indiana literature.[4] Among the most popular
writers were the poet James Whitcomb Riley and the novelist Booth
Tarkington. Riley's poetry recalled his rural and small-town childhood, portraying it as a bucolic and virtuous time. Tarkington be-
moaned Indianapolis's lost innocence as he watched the city discard
its traditional values. Even realistic writers like Theodore Dreiser

drew on their Indiana experiences to show how urban corruption and vice afflicted people.

For the more intellectually inclined residents, the sense of separateness became ideological alienation, a Hoosier version of populism. In the late nineteenth century, at the time of the agrarian protest movement in the country, the Populist Party voiced the political views of many farmers in Indiana and throughout the Midwest. The preamble to their 1892 party platform warned of a vast conspiracy being perpetrated by evil capitalists against farmers and workers. One young resident of Henry County and a graduate of DePauw University in Greencastle, Charles Beard, took the populist message to heart. Later, when he became a historian, he wrote *An Economic Interpretation of the Constitution of the United States* that traced the origins of that conspiracy.[5] He asserted that the founding fathers were businessmen who enshrined the protection of property in the Constitution. Restrained by the dictates of scholarship, Beard's conspiratorial interpretation was milder than those of other historians.

A more vociferous populism was expressed by the prominent Indiana socialist Eugene V. Debs, who was born and lived his entire life in Terre Haute. Like the Populists, Debs believed in a class struggle in which farmers and workers were exploited by greedy capitalists. As the Populists gained strength among farmers in mid-America, Debs helped strengthen the labor movement by playing a leading role in the Pullman Strike in 1894. Debs later garnered nearly a million votes as the Socialist Party presidential candidate in 1920 while imprisoned for protesting American involvement in World War I. Although his adversarial perspective was deeply embedded in Hoosier thinking, Debs's radical politics never attracted more than 6 percent of Indiana's conservative voters.

The Ku Klux Klan in the 1920s embodied the worst manifestation of Hoosier populism. Two themes were prominent in Klan propaganda: a patriotic glorification of America and Indiana and Protestant Christianity. Klansmen exploited the Hoosier self-image of exclusivity and transformed it into attacks on outsiders: Roman Catholics, the foreign born, and African Americans. By 1924, the Klan was sufficiently powerful to help elect Ed Jackson governor. But a year later the conviction of Grand Dragon D. C. Stephenson for assault and rape marked the end of Klan dominance.

Populism in all its forms was an outgrowth of an agrarian way of life that was being challenged by the lure of the cities. Increasingly, men and women were leaving farms for the economic opportunities and excitement of city life. The census of 1910 recorded a decline in the number of rural Hoosiers, and the census of 1920 reported that more of them were living in cities than on farms. Mechanization of agriculture and industrialization may have facilitated the migration, but Indiana lagged behind neighboring industrializing states such as Illinois and Ohio. And Indiana agriculture was still a man-behind-a-mule job. As late as 1920, only 4 percent of Indiana farmers had tractors.

Wherever Indianans lived in 1920, the population remained homogeneous: 95 percent were native born, 97 percent were white, and 75 percent were Protestant. They preferred to live in small towns and cities even when 51 percent of the population was urban. Even larger cities such as Indianapolis retained a small-town atmosphere. Meredith Nicholson reported that Indianapolis was a town "that became a city rather against its will,"[6] maintaining the highest percentage of single-family homes of any city in the country. With the exception of Gary, Nicholson describes other Indiana cities as "neighborly and cozy."[7] Poet James Whitcomb Riley best summarized the Hoosier attitude toward town life when he wrote, "You kin boast about yer cities, and their stiddy growth and size. . . . But the little Town of Tail-holt is big enough for me!"[8]

Covington, where Shoup grew up, was big enough for its inhabitants. Like many other small towns and cities throughout the state, it was a typical agricultural community with only the essential political, economic, and social services. The uniformity of town life enabled the Shoups to move from Ash Grove near Battle Ground to a farm in Foster near Covington, in 1916, without feeling uprooted. People there could trace their ancestry to the founding settlers in the early nineteenth century. Homogeneous like much of Indiana, it was a place where people were similar and looked familiar.

When Shoup lived in Covington, it was a small residential community, a retail trading center, and the county seat of Fountain County. There was some industry: a brick and cement factory, a canning factory, a saw mill, a grain elevator, and a gravel plant. But the city was primarily a service center for those who lived there and in the surrounding countryside. Downtown, the public square was lined with grocery stores, meat markets, dry goods stores, a department store, and other businesses. Two newspapers provided information, and knowledge and literature were housed in an "architectural gem," as the public library was known. Covington was connected to the outside world by the Big Four and Wabash railroads. The city provided electricity and bragged about its pure water.

For young David Shoup, the most important city service was its school system. He was age twelve when he enrolled in Covington

High School and was eager to meet the high standards set for students there. Two of his former classmates, Helen Van Doran Shelby and Genevieve Franklin Fette, remembered how "we went to school and we studied and there was no fooling around."[9] If students had grades of 90 percent or better, they were exempt from taking final exams. Shoup never had to take a final exam. As his mother once observed, "Even as a child he was determined to get to the top in whatever he did."[10] At a time when most Indiana schools just taught the basics, Shoup and his classmates were fortunate to have instruction in mathematics, French, physics, English, and history.

It was not all work and no play for Shoup and the class of 1921. Shoup played basketball, successfully ran for president of his senior class, and found time for a social life. At a Halloween party during his freshman year he met Zola De Haven. Shoup remembered how "within the very moment of this observation, I decided that this little girl was to be my wife and the mother of my children."[11] Their high school romance was troubled at times because they competed with one another for grades. Mrs. Shoup recalls always beating him in math and physics. But that rivalry did not discourage Shoup; other rivalries upset him. On one occasion, he was almost expelled from school for throwing a penny at a rival suitor during assembly. Years later, in 1931, the high school sweethearts were married.

After high school, Shoup went to DePauw University, primarily for financial reasons. He was awarded an Edward Rector Scholarship, a grant given to one hundred outstanding male graduates from Indiana high schools. The grant paid his tuition, but he still had to wait tables, wash dishes, work in a cement factory, and enroll in the Reserve Officers Training Corps (ROTC) to pay his living expenses. His financial problems proved so serious that he decided to take a year off after his junior year to teach school. A near fatal bout with pneumonia saw his savings go for hospital bills. After his yearlong leave of absence, Shoup returned to college. Majoring in math, he took every math course the college offered, including one on the theory of equations. Shoup helped organize and for a time chaired the math club and joined a fraternity, Delta Upsilon, which was a scholastic leader on campus. His academic record was impressive, and he narrowly missed making Phi Beta Kappa. Shoup also participated in extracurricular activities. He was on the track and rifle teams for four years and on the wrestling and football teams for two years. One of the highlights of his athletic career was winning the Indiana and Kentucky Amateur Athletic Union (AAU) marathon in 1925. Even with all these demands on his time, Shoup learned how to play and win at poker. Shoup's college experiences revealed his dogged determination and provided valuable lessons for a future officer who later shrewdly calculated military risks, endured physical hardships, and thrashed unwary gamblers.

Shoup left Indiana and joined the Marine Corps after he graduated from college. A year later he was in China, swept up in international events beyond anything he had ever imagined. But Shoup, like other Hoosiers, had not been isolated from the international and domestic forces that affected all Americans in the first two and half decades of the twentieth century. Everyone experienced progressivism, imperialism, World War I, and postwar disillusionment.

Shoup grew up at a time when the United States was emerging as a world power. His birth in 1904 coincided with the election of Theodore Roosevelt to a second term as president. Now an elected leader and not a president by default, Roosevelt personified the confident and assertive American nationalism. His second administration combined progressive reform at home with imperialism abroad. Above all, Roosevelt was enamored of power, which he exercised in unprecedented ways. In many respects he was the first strong president since Lincoln, and Americans were enthralled with his boisterous energy and enthusiasm.

Roosevelt's domestic program was both symbolic and substantive. Sometimes his initiatives were tentative or very modest, such as trust busting: at other times they were innovative and far reaching, such as conservation. But he was always concerned with power, extending public authority over private interests. In the Northern Securities case in 1902, for example, he signaled that there were limits to how far business consolidation could go. The Northern Securities Company had been organized by three financial titans, J. P. Morgan, E. H. Harriman, and James J. Hill, who created a huge railroad monopoly in the Northwest. Roosevelt responded by ordering the Justice Department to prosecute. In 1904, the Supreme Court ruled that the company had to be dismantled. Roosevelt was not against business consolidation per se, and at the time he tried to reassure Morgan that he was not launching a campaign to attack all trusts. But he objected to the arrogance of big business.

Roosevelt also objected to other presumptuous groups, including organized labor. When the United Mine Workers went on strike against the anthracite coal industry, Roosevelt intervened and asked both sides to accept federal arbitration. Later, during the presidential campaign of 1904, he claimed that he had worked out a "square deal" for both sides. Arguably, Roosevelt was anxious to curb the influence

to protect the public from private exploitation. He was against the trusts and supported additional railroad regulation. But Taft alienated the progressive faction of his party and ultimately allied himself with the conservative Republicans. His mishandling of the tariff issue and the progressive Republican attempt to unseat Speaker of the House Joe Cannon led to Taft's political demise. Taft did, however, extend the progressive movement by instituting more than twice the number of antitrust suits than Roosevelt; by sponsoring the Mann-Elkins Act, which enhanced the regulatory jurisdiction of the Interstate Commerce Commission; by endorsing a postal saving system; and by recommending campaign disclosure in the Publicity Act. Yet Taft failed to ride the crest of progressive reform and was caught in the undertow of his party's division.

In foreign affairs, Taft continued Roosevelt's policy of intervention in Latin America and the Open Door policy in the Far East.[13] He went further, however, by implementing a new form of intervention in both regions: Taft's "dollar diplomacy" encouraged American bankers to replace European creditors in the Caribbean and sponsored American investment in an international banking consortium in China to build a railroad.

Dollar diplomacy failed in both instances. In Latin America, the focus was on Nicaragua, as financial instability and political turmoil there appeared to threaten American interests. With the help of American businessmen in 1909, rebels deposed José Zaleya, a leader who was antagonistic to foreign penetration. His successor, Adolfo Diaz, was pro-American. He solicited support from the United States, and Secretary of State Knox obliged. In June 1911, Knox signed the Knox-Castrillo Convention by which, in exchange for funding the Nicaraguan debt with an American loan, Nicaragua would use its customs receipts as collateral and would accept American direction of its customs collection. Additionally, it granted the United States the right of intervention. The Knox-Castrillo Convention in effect turned Nicaragua into an American protectorate. Neither the U.S. Senate nor the Nicaraguan people accepted the accord. More revolutionary activity ensued, and Taft sent in the Marines in August 1912. In the end, dollar diplomacy gave way to the big stick.

Taft's policies were overshadowed by political blunders that led to a split in the Republican Party before the election of 1912. Roosevelt returned from hunting game in Africa to pursue a more challenging quarry, another term in the White House. The campaign turned into a duel between two candidates, Roosevelt and Woodrow Wilson, representing different forms of progressivism. Having split from the Republicans to form the Progressive (Bull Moose) Party, Roosevelt campaigned on his "New Nationalism," an advanced platform of reform that rested on vigorous federal governmental leadership. Wilson presented a more subdued reform agenda that anticipated only modest government action to reform the country in the areas of banking, tariff adjustment, and the dismemberment of monopolies.

Wilson's victory seemed to portend a limited domestic program. And for a time he confined himself to the three objectives he had announced in his campaign. His major victory was to overhaul the banking system with the Federal Reserve Act, which combined government and private administration and created a flexible monetary system. The Underwood Tariff was also a significant victory. It represented the first significant downward revision of the tariff since the Civil War and introduced the idea of an income tax. His efforts in antitrust legislation culminated in the Federal Trade Commission Act and the Clayton Antitrust Act, both of which signaled more government control over business consolidation. By 1914, these legislative accomplishments fulfilled Wilson's campaign promises, but a confluence of events that included a Republican comeback in the congressional elections, the demise of the Progressive Party, and Wilson's own sense of political necessity, led to a more ambitious reform effort.

One indication of Wilson's new attitude was his appointment of Louis Brandeis to the Supreme Court in January 1916, the first Jew on the high court and a renowned progressive. He followed this by supporting advanced progressive legislation such as rural credits, workmen's compensation for federal employees, and the restriction of child labor. By 1918, Wilson's record of domestic reform surpassed that of Roosevelt and Taft. In the end, like Roosevelt, he exerted strong executive leadership, enhancing the power of the presidency.

In foreign affairs he continued the interventionist approach of his predecessors.[14] Still a teacher at heart, his style of meddling was different. He felt compelled to teach Latin Americans a lesson in democracy. Using the Marines as instructors, he suppressed a revolution in Haiti in 1915, established a military government in the Dominican Republic in 1916, and secured the right to intervene in Nicaragua's domestic affairs. Wilson's most heavy-handed dealing was with Mexico. He refused to recognize the government of Victoriano Huerta and, in 1914, used a minor episode in Tampico as an excuse for seizing Vera Cruz. In 1916, Wilson ordered General John J. Pershing to invade Mexico in response to a Mexican attack on Americans led by Pancho

Villa. Like Roosevelt and Taft, Wilson used a big stick to discipline Latin Americans.

Wilson's greatest challenge in foreign affairs was the outbreak of World War I. When the war started and for three years thereafter, Wilson pursued a policy of neutrality. Economic and military factors, however, undermined that approach. Britain's mastery of the seas meant that the United States would either have to abandon virtually all trade or acquiesce to violations of American neutrality. Wilson chose the latter course, and the United States, albeit inadvertently, became the arsenal for the Entente powers. When their finances were exhausted, the United States became their creditor as well.

Economic ties alone would not have persuaded Wilson and the American public to go to war. The primary reason for the entrance of the United States into World War I was German submarine warfare. Starting in 1915, the Germans challenged Britain's supremacy on the seas by attacking without warning vessels destined for England. The sinking of the British liner *Lusitania* without warning resulted in the loss of American lives and outraged Wilson. He demanded the Germans stop the attacks, and for a time they acquiesced. Wilson wanted to avert war, and in 1916 he campaigned for reelection with the slogan "He kept us out of war." That boast lasted only until the Germans resumed unrestricted submarine warfare, with further loss of American life. The stage was set for a declaration of war, but Wilson did not use German tactics or violations of American neutrality as the rationale for declaring war. In April 1917, after German submarines attacked three American ships, he asked for a declaration of war "to end all wars," not just submarine attacks. Earlier that year, in January 1917, he presented to Congress his plan for the postwar world. He shared with them his vision of a permanent League of Nations to maintain peace and a world order based upon the principle of the self-determination of all nations. He called for a "peace without victory." Within months, America followed Wilson's idealistic crusade to fight for a new world order.

His war aims were elaborated on January 8, 1918, when he presented his Fourteen Points. They included postwar boundary adjustments, general principles of desirable international conduct, and most importantly, the creation of a League of Nations. At the peace conference in Versailles after the war, Wilson met stiff opposition to his Fourteen Points, ultimately bargaining away most of them to preserve the League. After winning the battle to keep the League, he returned home to face opposition to the League in the Senate. Led by Senator Henry Cabot Lodge, the Senate attached revisions and reservations to the treaty that Wilson could not accept. In the end, Wilson instructed his supporters to reject any compromise. He had decided to take the treaty fight to the people. Wilson then conducted an exhausting cross-country campaign to mobilize support for the treaty. But the strain was too much for him. He suffered a debilitating stroke that ended his campaign. The treaty fight was over.

Failure to join the League and realize the lofty Wilsonian war aims contributed to widespread national disillusionment. By 1920, the horrors of the world war, the failed peace, and a general demoralization seemed to pervade the country. Republican candidate Warren G. Harding captured the mood of the country when he told voters that what this country needed was a return to normalcy. He was not alone. In Indiana, Governor Warren T. McCray told the 1923 session of the General Assembly that "what the people of Indiana want is a season of government economy, and a period of legislative inaction and rest."[15] All over the country, Americans wanted to forget the passions of progressivism and ignore Wilsonian internationalism.

David Shoup grew up amid and was molded by the progressivism and imperialism that dominated the administrations of Theodore Roosevelt, Taft, and Wilson. He seems to have been most influenced by many of the rural progressives' battles with big business and their opposition to U.S. imperialism. Although Indiana's Senator Beveridge was both a leading progressive and a strident imperialist, many other midwestern senators, such as George Norris of Nebraska, simultaneously protested the injurious effect of business interests on U.S. foreign policy and the practice of American imperialism. Norris and other peace progressives like William Borah of Idaho dissented from U.S. interventionist policies and sought to conduct foreign relations in less obtrusive ways.[16] They were most influential in the years between 1919 and 1930, using their power on a number of occasions to implement their anti-imperialist ideology.[17] When the Coolidge administration decided to send marines to China in 1927 to protect American nationals, the peace progressives sharply protested the decision.[18]

Among the marines sent to China in 1927 was young second lieutenant Shoup. Like the peace progressives, he believed the deployment was unjustified and imperialistic. He complained in his journal "that China has many Americans, or those who propose to be Americans, inhabiting her country and in many cases exploiting her peoples. Yet they claim their right to protection from the U.S. some 10,000 miles away."[19] Furthermore, he did not believe that protecting American citizens was the reason for the deployment. Shoup shared the view of the Marine commanding general, Smedley Butler, that their true mission was to win a commercial war in China.[20]

Shoup's youthful skepticism about American foreign policy remained with him for the rest of his life. Later, at the time of the Vietnam War, he would question the motives behind the deployment of troops in Asia and voice the same complaint: American troops were being used inappropriately. That offended his Hoosier sensibilities, an outlook that embraced common sense and strong morals, which would guide him for the rest of his life.

Notes

1. *Commercial News*, November 13, 1960, 28.
2. *Indianapolis Star*, August 18, 1961.
3. James H. Madison, *The Indiana Way: A State History* (Bloomington, 1986).
4. Madison, *Indiana Way*, 187.
5. See Charles Beard, *An Economic Interpretation of the Constitution of the United States* (New York, 1913).
6. Quoted in *Indiana Way*, 177.
7. Madison, *Indiana Way*, 178.
8. Madison, *Indiana Way*, 179.
9. Mrs. Helen Van Doran Shelby and Mrs. Genevieve Franklin Fette, interview with the author, May 13, 1983.
10. *Indianapolis Star*, August 16, 1959.
11. Shoup MS Collection, Speech, November 11, 1960.
12. See Howard K. Beale, *Theodore Roosevelt and the Rise of America to World Power* (Baltimore, 1956).
13. See Walter V. Scholes and Marie V. Scholes, *The Foreign Policies of the Taft Administration* (Columbia, Mo., 1970).
14. See Arthur Link, *Woodrow Wilson* (New York, 1954).
15. Madison, *Indiana Way*, 289.
16. William E. Leuchtenburg, "Progressivism and Imperialism: The Progressive Movement and American Foreign Policy, 1898–1916," *Mississippi Valley Historical Review* 39, no. 3 (December 1952): 484.
17. Robert David Johnson, *The Peace Progressives and American Foreign Relations* (Cambridge, Mass., 1995), 2–3.
18. Johnson, *Peace Progressives*, 148.
19. David M. Shoup, *The Marines in China* (Hamden, Conn., 1987), 81.
20. Shoup, *Marines in China*, 110.

2

Marine in China

After graduation from college, Shoup had no career plans, and his decision to enter the Marine Corps was largely circumstantial. He joined DePauw's ROTC because "they paid you 30 cents a day for rations. . . . It came out to exactly $9 a month, which was exactly what I paid for my room rent, and in all truth that was the only reason I signed for the senior ROTC."[1] While he was in ROTC, a conference he attended with other cadets in the Scabbard and Blade Honor Society started him on his career with the Marines. At the conference, keynote speaker John A. Lejeune, major general commandant of the Marine Corps, encouraged the young men to seek a commission in the Corps if they were honor graduates at their colleges. All Lejeune required was a personal letter expressing interest. Shoup decided to apply and was later offered a commission.

In the interim, Shoup, who desperately needed money, learned that he would be well paid if he went on active duty in the Army Reserve Corps. He remembered that, "due to my financial status, which hovered around the zero point all my life up to this point, I got active duty at Camp Knox (Kentucky) for a two-week period as Army Reserve Corps. . . . Every time I could get two more weeks' active duty, I took it, because I got good pay, more money than I ever saw in my life."[2] While he was at Camp Knox, from May to August 1926, the Marine Corps asked him to report to Chicago for a physical examination. He incorrectly assumed that the Corps would pay his travel expenses and later claimed that, had he known he would have to pay his own way, he never would have gone for that physical. But he did go, subsequently accepted a commission as a second lieutenant in the Marine Corps, and resigned his commission in the army.

Shoup reported for duty at the Marine Corps barracks in Philadelphia on August 25, 1926, to take his oath and receive his orders. On his first day in the Corps he made his first mistake when he learned that his assignment included playing football. Shoup objected, saying, "Sir, I didn't come to the Marine Corps to play football."[3] Major Rorex ordered Shoup to stand at attention for what seemed an eternity. "From now on," Major Rorex barked, "the Marine Corps will tell you what to do; you're not going to tell us what you do."[4] Shoup played football and attended Basic School.

His training and football playing were soon cut short by a fortuitous turn of events. As he returned to his barracks on April 1, 1927, the Officer of the Day informed him that he was one of ten in his class at Basic School ordered to go to China. Shoup dismissed the news as an April Fool's prank until he was shown the list of assigned officers. Minutes later his good news was confirmed by jealous classmates. When he peered into one noisy room, "A half dozen merciless hands grabbed me, dragged me into this room with its unbearable stench of cigarette smoke and alcohol, and threw me to the floor pouring Gordon's gin upon me from head to foot."[5] Now properly baptized for overseas duty, Shoup joined nine others on their way to China to protect American lives and property in a country locked in civil war.

Shoup's mission to China was the first of many instances in his career when he was swept up in the current of a rapidly changing world. At times his role was a minor one, like this first tour of duty in China. At a later date he played a more central part in a Far East war. In 1927, the young lieutenant found himself part of a contingent of marines sent to protect Americans from Chinese rebels who were attacking foreigners. Though a very modest response by the Coolidge administration, it was symbolic of the Open Door policy that was central to American Far East policy for twenty-eight years.

American imperialists with dreams of a vast Chinese market and missionaries with visions of saving Chinese souls had inspired the formulation of the Open Door policy in 1899 and 1900. With the seizure of the Philippines following the Spanish-Cuban-American War, what was fanciful became real. The United States was now a colonizing power in the Far East, and China looked more enticing. The opportunity to participate in the exploitation of China had emerged three years before war with Spain. The Sino-Japanese war in 1895 gave victorious Japan a singular opportunity to dominate China. European powers with commercial interests in China feared that would happen and rushed to create economic enclaves in China. Spheres of economic and political influence were carved by Germany in the

Shan-tung peninsula and by Russia in the Liaotung peninsula. France established a naval base at Kwangchowan, and Britain, which already controlled most of China's trade and investment, secured new concessions on the Shan-tung peninsula.

The scramble for spheres of influence prompted Britain to explore ways to prevent further expansion of concessions at the expense of Chinese sovereignty and to prevent economic rivalry between the countries establishing spheres of influence. The British were aware that the United States wanted access but did not want to establish its own domain in China. Consequently, the British suggested to the McKinley administration that the two nations issue a joint declaration supporting equal trade and respecting Chinese sovereignty. McKinley refused at first but later incorporated those principles in a unilateral declaration.

William Rockhill, an expert on China, approached Secretary of State John Hay with a suggestion formulated by an Englishman, Chinese customs officer Alfred Hippisley. His document was sent to Hay and McKinley and, virtually unaltered, it became the first Open Door note of 1899. The note asked each foreign power in China to allow other countries to trade within their sphere, but it accepted those spheres as legitimate, thus infringing upon Chinese sovereignty. One year later, at the time of the Boxer Rebellion, a second Open Door note was sent. The occasion was the aftermath of an uprising by Chinese militants, the Society of Righteous and Harmonious Fists (Boxers) who attacked Christian missionaries and Chinese Christians and laid siege to the diplomatic compounds in Peking. The United States contributed twenty-five hundred troops to an international expedition that liberated the legations. Concerned that the foreign troops might remain after suppressing the rebellion, Secretary Hay sent a second note to foreign powers in China with an appeal to respect Chinese sovereignty. But no reprisals were threatened. Neither note included a provision for enforcement. Consequently, both were ignored.

American intentions in China in 1899 and 1900 appeared noble, but in reality there was no strong commitment to protect anyone. The United States wanted to pry open the door of opportunity for American merchants and missionaries. In time, merchants, missionaries, and diplomats formed an Open Door constituency, which by the 1920s significantly influenced American policy toward China.

For more than a decade, the Open Door policy went unchallenged. Then, after the fall of the Manchu dynasty in 1911, it was threatened. China was in turmoil. The country was under the nominal rule of a politician, General Yuan Shih-Kai, but he had no control over regional warlords, who ruled their own fiefdoms. Civil war raged across the country, turning China into a battleground where no one was safe, including foreign residents. These disturbances persisted until World War II, necessitating a change in policy. The Open Door policy was replaced with militancy. From 1911 to 1941, there was an American military presence in China that included an Army infantry regiment and gunboats along the Yangtze reinforced by destroyers and cruisers off the coast. Marines were garrisoned in Shanghai and guarded the legation in Peking, the international settlement, and the railway to the capital.

Before World War I, the Chinese revolution posed no immediate danger, and for many troops stationed there it was an enjoyable assignment. Marine officers who were at the Legation Quarter, for example, had servants. Even enlisted men could hire laborers to cook and clean. Their military responsibilities were often constabulary or ceremonial, leaving ample time to participate in the social life of the diplomatic quarter and explore the exotic diversions of the capital. After World War I, marines and other military personnel found China less entertaining. From 1922 to 1925, escalating civil unrest and rampaging Chinese soldiers threatened American lives and property. Faced with a mounting crisis, American foreign policy had to be changed.

A reconsideration of American foreign policy in China became more urgent as events accelerated in 1925. Starting with the Shanghai incident of May 30, antiforeign agitation in China intensified. The episode originated in a labor dispute in Shanghai mills. A strike at the Nagai Wata Mill led to a riot and police firing on strikers. Students joined laborers on May 30 at a memorial service for one of the strikers. The police intervened, and a confrontation between them and a crowd of about two hundred led to twelve Chinese deaths and seventeen wounded. News of the May 30 incident spread quickly and provoked demonstrations all across the country, directed at all foreigners but focused especially on the Japanese and British.[6]

One of the more serious incidents occurred at Han Chow when an angry mob invaded the British Concession on June 11 and attacked police and members of the Municipal Council. Despite the landing of British sailors, the riot continued and Chinese were killed and wounded as the British attempted to quell the disturbance. In Han Chow and elsewhere, demonstrators railed against the hated unequal treaties.

The unequal treaties had been imposed on China in the middle of the nineteenth century. In 1842 and 1843, the British negotiated treaties that guaranteed them most-favored-nation treatment and extraterritoriality; that is, British subjects accused of crimes had to be tried by their own diplomatic officials, not by Chinese courts. A year later the United States also secured most-favored-nation treatment and extraterritoriality in the Treaty of Wanghsia. Later, the treaty system was expanded in response to the Taiping Rebellion, which started in 1850 and lasted fifteen years. The rebellion and the refusal of the Chinese government to comply with the treaties of 1842–1844 persuaded British and American diplomats to secure revision of the treaties. Finally, in June 1858, France and Russia joined Britain and the United States in imposing the Treaties of Tientsin. Under the terms of these treaties, China opened eleven ports and allowed legations at Peking, trade, Christian missions in the interior, a customs service under a foreign administrator, and legalization of the opium trade. Basically, the Treaties of Tientsin left China without control of its economy or protection from exploitation.[7]

Neither the Open Door notes nor the Nine-Power Treaty effectively eliminated the abuses of the unequal treaties. In 1925 and later, the elimination of those treaties was the rallying cry of Chinese revolutionaries. Some consideration, therefore, had to be given to treaty revision while protecting American lives and property. After the Shanghai incident, the State Department responded to public opinion in the United States. They recognized that the time had come to honor the agreements made at the Washington Conference. The treaty powers at the conference had agreed to convene a Commission on Extraterritoriality and a Special Conference on the Chinese Customs Tariff within three months after the conference ended and three months after the effective date of the tariff treaty. Internal strife in China had made discussions impractical. Then, in 1925, the pressure of events persuaded Secretary of State Frank Kellogg to issue a public statement. Two months after the opening session of the Special Tariff Conference, he told an audience at the Council on Foreign Relations in New York,

> I have every hope that the aspiration of China to regain the control over her tariffs and to establish the jurisdiction of her courts over foreigners living within her borders will be worked out by the Conference with the assistance of the Commission on Extraterritoriality.[8]

Secretary Kellogg's position was now clear. He believed the Special Tariff Conference and Commission on Extraterritoriality should be convened to abolish the unequal treaty system. Kellogg was supported by one vocal segment of American public opinion, Protestant missionary societies. By 1925, there were between four thousand and five thousand American Protestant missionaries in China, protected by the toleration clauses in the Sino-American treaties of 1858 and 1903. Basically, the treaties provided that Christians, both American and Chinese, would not be persecuted because of their faith. Also, by both treaty and tradition, missionaries had the right to own land. Understandably, missionaries in China and their supporters in the United States had a keen interest in American policy toward China, and they endorsed Kellogg's proposed changes in policy. In July 1925, Farnell P. Turner, secretary of the Foreign Missions Conference of North America, which represented ninety-eight Protestant societies in the United States, sent a letter to Secretary Kellogg stating, "We are gratified that our own Government has taken the lead . . . to frame a new policy towards China, as suggested in the Nine Power Treaty."[9] His sentiment was typical of missionary organizations, which were beginning to form a pro-China lobby.

Some commentators disagreed with the missionaries' wishes. One critic was Rodney Gilbert, an American journalist who wrote for the British *North China Daily News and Herald*. Gilbert attacked missionary influence on American public opinion. He suggested, in June 1926, that missionaries in south China who were sympathetic to the Kuomintang movement might quickly change their minds, and that if they should do so, American policy would change. "If the missionary cause is seriously threatened," Gilbert argued, "missionary unions can move Americans on gunboats and bring them into lively action when no other force can make them shift their moorings. A change in missionary attitude, therefore, means, in the first place, that the tide of unspeakable drool which has been going home for a year about China's rights and aspirations will be abruptly stemmed in both America and England."[10] He went on to say that missionaries had the power to shape public opinion in the United States and encourage intervention in China.[11] Gilbert may have exaggerated missionary influence, but his views had a profound impact on one young marine heading to China.

What missionaries or anyone else thought about treaty revision was set aside after the Nanking incident of March 24, 1927. At that moment, the immediate concern was whether the United States should intervene in China. Reports to the State Department from the American consul in Nanking, John K. Davis, indicated that retreating northern troops were trapped in the city by nationalist troops. While they were there, the northern troops looted, destroyed property, and attacked foreigners. Davis, caught in the melee, assembled those seeking refuge and took them to the Standard Oil property. When the situation worsened, Davis signaled for help from American and British warships. They responded by sending landing parties ashore and laying down a barrage of fire. Davis and his group managed to escape to the warships.

After his escape, Consul Davis notified the State Department on March 29 that he believed those Chinese attacking foreigners were not northern soldiers but troops of the advancing Kuomintang army. An American minister in China, John Van Antwerpt MacMurray, shared Davis's view and cabled the State Department that pressure must be exerted on the Kuomintang government. Additionally, he advocated that Americans in Kuomintang territory be evacuated; once done, all Chinese ports from Shanghai south should be blockaded. When Secretary of State Kellogg received MacMurray's message, he replied that he wanted to have Admiral Williams's advice first.

Admiral Clarence S. Williams, commander-in-chief of the United States Asiatic Fleet, had been ordered to China to protect Americans. Williams shared MacMurray's view that women and children should be evacuated from north China and that those who remained should be protected by sending additional troops to Tientsin.[12] Williams suggested that the fifteen hundred marines en route to Shanghai be diverted to Tientsin, that a brigade be readied to sail if needed, and that additional troops at division strength be sent and held in reserve in the Philippines. The State Department disagreed and followed the advice of the United States War Department, which in an April 5 memorandum concluded that the forces in Tientsin and Peking were adequate to protect nationals from mob violence. The State Department further maintained that it would take fifty thousand troops to defend Peking and Tientsin. Kellogg therefore replied to the minister and the admiral that, in addition to the thirteen hundred marines and soldiers at Peking, fifteen hundred marines could be transported from Shanghai to north China if needed, fifteen hundred more could be added, and an additional regiment of two hundred might be available from the Philippines.

Williams conferred with the newly arrived Marine commander, Brigadier General Smedley D. Butler, and they agreed that marine reinforcements were necessary. Williams then asked for two battalions of the Sixth Regiment, an artillery battalion, two aircraft squadrons, a brigade headquarters, and a service company. This more modest request was granted. He was reminded, however, that his mission remained the same. His force was to protect lives by evacuating Americans from the interior and to protect private property only if lives were endangered. American forces were to cooperate with the forces of other foreign powers, but no joint military action was authorized.

The marines sent to China were prepared to fight, but only when it was absolutely necessary. It was assumed that their forbearance would win the respect of the Chinese, and their independent but cooperative relationship with the foreign units would encourage them to follow the American example. It was a difficult assignment. And young Second Lieutenant David Shoup was on his way to carry out that challenging mission. He was part of a group of marines made up of 76 officers and 1,443 enlisted men under the command of Colonel M. C. Davis. They were to ship out from San Diego for the Philippines and later depart for China. Shoup's contingent consisted of the Second Battalion, Tenth Regiment (artillery), Fifth Company Engineers, and a Light Tank platoon.

When Shoup arrived in San Diego he contacted his brother Daniel, who lived in Redlands, and was pleasantly surprised to learn that Daniel could visit him before he embarked. After spending an enjoyable few hours with his brother, David Shoup had the impression that "all these warlike preparations brought back memories of his days in the A.E.F. [Allied Expeditionary Force] and I feel sure that, without his home ties, very little persuasion would have been necessary to cause him to go with us. Something in his temperament just seemed to tell me that he wanted to go. No matter how tough had been his days in France, the spell of the service showed through it all."[13] David admired his older brother, who had once predicted that a war with Japan was inevitable. Now that admiration was returned. As Shoup was about to leave country and family behind, he reflected, "It's not what you're going to, or what you're goin' to find. It's those things *you have to do*, and the folks you leave behind. That's what makes going any place kinda tough."[14]

Shoup soon learned just how tough the going could be on his first sea voyage. But he survived the seasickness and arrived in healthy condition at Olangapo in the Philippines. Once there, he spent time painting and cleaning equipment, attending "schools not requiring strenuous exercise,"[15] and training with his machine gun company. He also enjoyed himself at bars, where he could drink in public. Back home, Prohibition meant drinking secretly. On occasion he and his buddies frequented the Santa Ana, self-proclaimed to be the "largest cabaret in the world."[16] Shoup observed, "It is here that hundreds of ballerinas lend themselves to the fine art of shaking the hoofs. Just guessing, but I might say that perhaps some not only lend themselves, but sell and shake, other than the hoofs." Apparently Shoup enjoyed the Philippines.

His stay in the Philippines ended on June 10, when he boarded the *Chamount* for Shanghai, arriving there the same day. As soon as he arrived, he sensed the excitement. "Everything was bristling, just waiting for the match to touch off the fireworks, for when troops are being trained to fight and taught to expect it, they become impatient with waiting and marking time."[17] But he had misgivings about the role he and his fellow marines were about to play. Shoup thought "that China has many Americans, or those who propose to be Americans, inhabiting her country and in many cases exploiting her peoples. Yet they claim their right to protection from the U.S. some 10,000 miles away."[18] Shoup was not alone. There were other observers who were ambivalent about Americans in China.

To some extent, Shoup's negative attitude toward Americans in China was based on his reading of Rodney Gilbert's book *What's Wrong with China* (1926). Shoup recorded in his journal long passages from the book, including Gilbert's unflattering categorization of American residents. Shoup cites Gilbert's view that "the missionaries misrepresent conditions in China to justify their own continued existence and residence in the country. . . . The commercial agent in China misrepresents conditions to keep his job . . . [and the] diplomat tones down his reports and misrepresents conditions in China chiefly because he enjoys a quiet pleasant life." Shoup's own view was that of these three groups, the missionaries "as a class . . . are perhaps the richest. They own great buildings and lands and are great money lenders."[19] Above all, Shoup was appalled by the exploitation.

American expatriates were not the only thing Gilbert found wrong in China. Shoup cites Gilbert's belief that "China has never in her history had such a thing as government by the consent of the governed . . . but with each new dynasty the land, and the people on the face of it, have been the prizes awarded to the champion in a free-for-all fight. . . . The Chinese people have always been docile under discipline, even when cruelly severe and unreasonable, and have always been unruly and insubordinate when 'given their own head.'"[20] Perhaps everything was wrong with China. Shoup had to find that out for himself, so he began his explorations of Shanghai. His first impressions were limited by his experiences during shore patrol, when he discovered the cabarets and other establishments marines visited on liberty. He wanted to see more of the city, particularly the Chinese section. On one patrol, Shoup did manage to enter the Chinese quarter only to discover his presence there was not welcome. Surrounded by an angry mob, Shoup learned that his being armed was a violation of protocol. More important, a bystander who spoke English said he was mistaken for a "Britisher." Shoup reflected in his journal that the mob's reaction "portrays the attitude of the Chinese toward the British. They have caused this by their ill treatment of the Chinese, I have seen them throw the rickshaw coolies' clackers [coins] in the gutter or give him none and strike them across the face with a swagger stick. All Marines were drilled and cautioned to be envoys of good will, and any transgression from proper treatment of the natives was not tolerated."[21] Better informed, the next time Shoup visited the Chinese section, he went in civilian clothes and hid his weapon in his shirt.

Shoup's Shanghai adventures ended on July 5, when his battalion was sent to Tientsin. With Shanghai stabilized, Admiral Williams, army Brigadier General Joseph Costner, and Minister MacMurray considered other vulnerable areas. Fearful that Nationalist troops might move farther north to Tientsin and Peking, they asked the State Department for more troops to protect the northern cities. The State Department concurred and requested that the Navy Department send more warships and marines to China. Anticipating reinforcements, General Butler divided his marines between Shanghai and Tientsin in July. Those going to Tientsin had the delicate task of simultaneously cooperating with and restraining the military forces of the foreign powers. Allies were needed to help protect Americans, not to intervene in Chinese affairs. Protecting MacMurray, who refused to leave Peking, complicated the Marines' assignment. The entire responsibility encompassed defending Americans in Tientsin, protecting the Tientsin-Peking railroad, and possibly rescuing the American legation at Peking.

Under these circumstances Butler worked closely with other commanders in the region and sent staff members to joint combat conferences. For the duration of 1927 and 1928, Butler divided his time between preparing his troops to mobilize on short notice, cooperating with foreign commanders, and negotiating with the leaders of opposing Nationalist and northern armies. Increasingly, however, most of his time was spent restraining the Japanese. Shoup noticed how "the Japs play a peculiar role in Chinese affairs. . . . If they can get the Chinese worried and then take advantage of them in some way that is a supreme delight."[22]

Butler kept a watchful eye on his marines in the Tientsin area. On July 27, Butler inspected Shoup's outfit at Camp MacMurray and explained their mission in China. Shoup recalled that "at this talk, he again impressed upon us that we . . . are now individual diplomats serving the U.S. Government in gaining the good will of the whole of China [and] will be the greatest assets possible in . . . this real . . . commercial war."[23] Butler asserted that American trade with China had increased by $27 million since the coming of the Marines, and Shoup found "very interesting . . . his explanation of the type of Americans in China who are doing all the growling and paying no taxes in the U.S. and are receiving $3,500 worth of protection per person."[24] Like General Butler, Shoup believed marines were in China to protect U.S. business interests at a great cost. Shoup did not think it was worth the price and wondered "what really is our mission here and of what benefit we are to the promotion of civilization."[25] Perhaps, Shoup mused, "The nations of the world [should] accept the situation as is and contrive some systematic method of developing China . . . to a point where she is able to know and understand her own needs as a nation."[26] In any event, Shoup recognized that Japan had to be prevented from interfering in China. Because they are "making no effort to conceal their helpful attitude toward the Northerners, it may be but a few generations until the Japanese school children will see the Urals as the western boundary of their Empire."[27] Like his brother, Shoup sensed that one day Japan's ambitions would lead to war with the United States.

As far as the current situation in China was concerned, Shoup grasped why undisciplined Chinese soldiers attacked foreigners in Nanking and elsewhere. His chance meeting with a northern soldier who spoke English was a revelation. Shoup wrote in his journal,

> I asked when he was last paid, at which he slowly shook his head, looked pitifully to earth, and remarked that his last pay was received Chinese New Year Day, and at that time he had received twenty cents (about nine cents gold). This day is in February some time and it was then the latter part of July. Being curious to know just what sort of fighting spirit could be maintained under these conditions, I asked him if he had done any fighting during that time. He glanced at me in a rather knowing manner and said, 'Twenty cents worth, sir.' This speaks the attitude of thousands of Chinese soldiers and helps one to understand the cause for such as the "Nanking Outrage" and the actions of an unfed, unpaid, unclothed, and undisciplined army of mentally starved soldiers and their policy of loot, plunder, and rape.[28]

Shoup was convinced that Americans had no conception of the conditions in China that led to the attacks on foreigners.

Shoup's brief but illuminating encounter with this Chinese soldier relieved the daily monotony of hikes and drills. His soldiering remained uneventful until October, when he became seriously ill. Shoup recovered slowly, and while he was in the hospital he learned on December 16 that he was going home. Before he left, he was stationed in Shanghai, where he watched foreign troops leave China. One day he witnessed the ceremonious departure of the British defense force, the Green Howard. In a display of solidarity with their comrades in arms, the British presented the Fourth Regiment Marines with a bagpipe. The Marines reciprocated by playing the bagpipes as the Green Howard boarded their ship. Shoup was unmoved. He believed that "the British policy and method of treating and handling the Chinese is one quite in contrast with that of our own. And at times it appears that an iron-handed, domineering, bullying attitude is born and bred into the 'Tommies.'"[29] With much less fanfare than the British departure, Shoup left China on January 7, 1928.

Shoup left China convinced that the U.S. presence there was an intrusion. He believed the Chinese people should be allowed to determine their own destiny without foreign interference. He also shared General Butler's view that American residents in China were undeserving of military protection. Only China, Shoup reflected, deserved protection from the imperial designs of countries like Japan.

Three years after Shoup left China, Japan's aggressive intentions there were evident. Alleging that the railway explosion at Mukden on September 18, 1931, was an attack, Japanese forces seized the local arsenal. Later, Japanese troops expanded their operation to include the seizure of the three eastern provinces. By February 1932, the Japanese set up a puppet government of Manchukuo. Secretary of State Stimson notified all signatories of the nine-power pact that the United States would not recognize the new country. Subsequently the League of Nations adopted the Stimson nonrecognition formula.

Nothing dissuaded the Japanese. And in the years following their takeover in Manchuria, the Japanese reaffirmed their intentions to dominate China. In April 1934, a spokesman for the Japanese Foreign Office, Eliji Amau, asserted that his country had a special mission and responsibilities in east Asia. The meaning of the obscure pronouncement was later clarified. Ambassador Hirosi Saito in May met with Secretary of State Cordell Hull with an eight-point proposal. The key point was the suggestion that Japan and the United States divide the Pacific into two spheres of influence. Japan would dominate the western Pacific and the United States would dominate the eastern Pacific. Hull recognized immediately that Japan wanted to nullify the Open Door policy, since China would be in Japan's sphere. He rejected Saito's plan.

Shoup returned to China in 1934, when Japan was declaring its special rights and responsibilities. His assignment was to coach the post pistol and rifle teams while performing other legation guard duties in Peking. Shoup was a successful coach. His pistol team won a major competition. Otherwise, his duty was uneventful, leaving him free to enjoy the active social life of the capital with his wife. He also had time to observe the Japanese. Years later, when he was training American troops to fight the Japanese, he shared his experience with Japanese troops in China. He recounted how he had once seen Japanese soldiers return from a forced march on a hot, dusty summer day with their canteens full. Shoup recalled, "If a Japanese officer said one swallow, they took just one swallow. That's discipline."[30]

His second tour was cut short by illness in 1936. As he was leaving China, he saw trains filled with Japanese soldiers. He did not know it at the time, but Japan was mobilizing for war with China. One year later the Japanese attacked, and the Sino-Japanese war ensued. Four years later Shoup would return to the Far East, this time to fight an enemy he knew he would have to meet on the battlefield.

Shoup's tours of duty in China made a lasting impression on him. As a young second lieutenant in 1927, he observed that the Chinese were weak, incapable of self-government, and easy prey to foreign exploitation. He questioned American motives in China as well. In his journal he cites Rodney Gilbert's observation that, "the American 'holier-than-thou' attitude in the Orient is a policy founded upon nothing but hypocrisy leading to nothing but dissension of which all are ready to take every advantage."[31] Shoup shared that view and remained skeptical about American intentions in China and other countries in the Far East for the rest of his life.

Thirty-nine years later, in a May 1966 speech protesting American involvement in Vietnam, he referred to his assignments in China. He told an audience at Pierce College, from "my experiences over parts of five years in China and what I know of conditions there today, I am sure that more Chinese know where tomorrow's food is coming from than ever [before]. . . . And to what must go the credit? The system they're serving under. The alienation of the friendship of the great and wonderful Chinese people will surely vie for decades to come as the greatest blunder that this country ever made in their relations with other nations, unless the final results from our Vietnam commitment overshadow it."[32] Although he originally believed the Chinese incapable of self-government, he later concluded they successfully empowered themselves. And he maintained the Vietnamese should do the same. On both occasions, when Shoup was in China and later when he attacked the American intrusion in Vietnam, he avowed the wisdom of allowing nations to choose their own governments.

Notes

1. John Luter, interview with General David M. Shoup, August 29, 1972, Washington, D.C., Oral History Research Office, Columbia University, 11.
2. Luter interview of Shoup, 12–13.
3. Luter interview of Shoup, 15.
4. Luter interview of Shoup, 15.
5. Shoup, *Marines in China*, 23.
6. Dorothy Borg, *American Policy and the Chinese Revolution, 1925–1928* (New York, 1947), 23.
7. Warren I. Cohen, *America's Response to China* (New York, 1980), 25.
8. Quoted in Borg, *American Policy*, 67.
9. Borg, *American Policy*, 70.
10. Borg, *American Policy*, 92.
11. Borg, *American Policy*, 92.
12. Borg, *American Policy*, 367.
13. Shoup, *Marines in China*, 39.
14. Shoup, *Marines in China*, 40.
15. Shoup, *Marines in China*, 54.
16. Shoup, *Marines in China*, 64.
17. Shoup, *Marines in China*, 79–80.
18. Shoup, *Marines in China*, 81.
19. Quotes in Shoup, *Marines in China*, 82–83.
20. Shoup, *Marines in China*, 82–83.
21. Shoup, *Marines in China*, 83–84.
22. Shoup, *Marines in China*, 86.
23. Shoup, *Marines in China*, 93.
24. Shoup, *Marines in China*, 110.
25. Shoup, *Marines in China*, 110.
26. Shoup, *Marines in China*, 116.
27. Shoup, *Marines in China*, 116.
28. Shoup, *Marines in China*, 116.
29. Shoup, *Marines in China*, 117–18.
30. Shoup, *Marines in China*, 143.
31. Shoup, *Marines in China*, 84.
32. "Remarks by General David M. Shoup, U.S. Marine Corps (Retired) at the 10th Annual Junior College World Affairs Day, Pierce College, Los Angeles, California," *Congressional Record*, Senate, February 20, 1967.

3

Tarawa

Near the end of Shoup's tour of duty in China, he contracted pneumonia. His physician had difficulty bringing down his fever and ordered him home for additional medical treatment. As Shoup was leaving northern China in 1936, he saw that his train was filled with Japanese soldiers, an ominous sign of mounting tension between Japan and China. Even more disturbing was an episode that occurred during his layover in Tokyo. A taxi driver seeing Shoup in uniform told him, "We fight you someday."[1] He was right. Shoup was destined to fight Japanese soldiers.

A year later a minor clash between Japanese and Chinese troops at the Marco Polo Bridge near Peking on July 7, 1937, escalated into war. The Roosevelt administration responded by sending twelve hundred marines to Shanghai on August 17. Roosevelt went further on October 5, when he appealed to Americans to recognize the dangers of aggression and the need to quarantine aggressor nations. Although the timing of his speech suggests he had Japan in mind, he quickly retreated from his bold appeal when the American public adamantly rejected the quarantine speech. His next step was more cautious. He suggested that the signatories of the Nine-Power Treaty meet to consider a response. But when the powers convened in Brussels, no one was prepared to take decisive action.

At a time when Congress responded to the public mood by passing so-called neutrality legislation that hampered the president's ability to react to international crises, Roosevelt could do nothing. It took the outbreak of war in Europe to embolden Roosevelt. After a year of inaction following its defeat of Poland, Germany resumed its lightning warfare, overrunning Denmark, Norway, Belgium, Holland, and northern France. Recognizing the imminent danger to the

United States if Germany controlled the Atlantic sea-lanes, preventing aid to Britain, Roosevelt ordered the Sixth Marines, increased to brigade strength, to assist the British garrison in Iceland.

In 1941, Shoup was promoted to major and served in the Headquarters Company of the First Provisional Marine Brigade in Iceland. While he was there, the Japanese bombed Pearl Harbor. Shoup purposely waited ten days to sort out his emotions before writing to his wife. When he wrote, he expressed deep sorrow over the loss of life in Hawaii, but avowed that the attack had been necessary to unify the country.[2] It was shameful, he later wrote, that the United States had been so short-sighted. Earlier lack of military preparation now meant that taking back Guam and Wake Island would require a hundred times more manpower. Equally disturbing to Shoup was the missed opportunity to appropriate funds to rebuild the defenses of Guam. Now the price would be paid in blood.[3]

With the United States at war, Shoup was quickly reassigned. He went first to Camp Elliott in San Diego to be an operations and training officer (G3) for the Second Marine Division, and he continued to serve in that capacity when the division was sent to New Zealand in 1942. He was promoted to lieutenant colonel and temporarily assigned to the First Marine Division as an observer in Guadalcanal, followed by a similar assignment with the Forty-third Infantry Division in Rendova where he was wounded in action and evacuated. Shoup then rejoined General Julian C. Smith's staff as G3 (operations officer) and masterminded the planning for the assault on Betio Island, Tarawa atoll, Gilbert Islands, in central Micronesia.

The battle of Tarawa was Shoup's finest hour as a combat officer in the Marine Corps. His heroic actions during the assault on Betio Island were the culmination of fourteen years of service in a variety of assignments that often seemed unrelated to the task of leading troops into harm's way. On his first day in the Marines when he had the temerity to question his orders to play football, Shoup received his first lesson in obeying orders and the first of several assignments to participate on Corps teams. Apparently, his superiors believed that marines who won on the playing fields and rifle ranges of military bases would win battles.

Playing football was followed by other assignments in Corps athletics. He coached the football and wrestling squads when on board the USS *Maryland* in 1930; directed the post boxing team and a boxing squad of fifteen lieutenants of the Thirty-second Chinese Army when he was assigned to the Marine Detachment at the American Legation in Peking, China in 1934–1935; and while in China he coached a pistol team that won the 1935 Asiatic Division Rifle and Pistol Competitions.

His greatest personal success in Corps athletics was in marksmanship. When he returned to the United States in 1937, he was stationed at Marine Barracks, Puget Sound Navy Yard, in Bremerton, Washington, where he did guard duty and trained marines and Navy personnel at the rifle range. He was also a member of the rifle and pistol team. The team captain, Carey A. Randall (later major general), recalled that, "At that time he was not a good shooter. . . . He was a miserable shot when he started . . . I would have to classify him as a sharp shooter at best. But because of his determination to learn how to do it properly . . . he later on became a distinguished marksman, which is as high with a pistol as you can go. That meant that he had qualified in the very top category three years in a row in Marine Corps matches."[4]

In addition to athletics, Shoup excelled in all his other duties. Without exception, he received high praise from all his commanders in his fitness reports. His first report, by Colonel H. C. Snyder, noted, "His manner and bearing and general conduct have been such as to mark him as a very promising young officer."[5] Those that followed expressed the same opinion. Shoup's grades on all aspects of his performance were consistently between 3 and 4 on a four-point scale. Later, when a descriptive grid was used, he was rated as either outstanding or excellent, the two highest ratings. Shoup always received high marks in leadership ("the capacity to direct, control, and influence others and still maintain high morale") and force ("the faculty of carrying out with energy and resolution that which is believed to be reasonable, right, or duty").[6]

Those who served under Shoup found him demanding. General William K. Jones was a second lieutenant in 1939, when he first met Captain Shoup, who was his tactics instructor. Jones remembers that Shoup's "no-nonsense approach and his absolute insistence on our knowing our assigned lessons, his scathing humor and criticism . . . made us all scared to death of him."[7] Yet Shoup could be entertaining as well. Subsequently, when Jones served under Shoup at Camp Elliott, he remembered that "one day he [Shoup] came out of his tent and put something up on his bulletin board . . . he said, 'Hey, Bill. Come over here. I want you to see something. I got this request for Headquarters Marine Corps to nominate three lieutenants to go to Monmouth [Army Signal School] . . . and I arranged them in the proper order and here is the message I sent to them. I just said, Lovett, Petit, and Pricket.'"[8] To Jones, the episode demonstrated that Shoup, "as stern and as sometimes as tactless as he could be in his official dealings, had a great sense of humor and could always see the funny side of things."[9]

The real test of Shoup's ability came during the war. Before the battle of Tarawa, officers who served with him saw how he skillfully managed his superiors. Brigadier General F. Paul Henderson recalled that when he was with Shoup in New Zealand, Shoup "knew how to keep top brass happy, tell them what he thought they ought to know but don't tell them what they didn't need to get their nose in . . . one of the things he was very strong on there at that time was checking on regimental and battalion commanders and people like that. He very soon pretty well figured out who really had it and who should take a regiment or battalion into combat and who shouldn't. And, in some way he managed to persuade the Division to relieve them, give them other jobs or whatever and get the right sort of people in. That's one thing he was very, very strong on."[10] Shoup's consummate managerial skills enabled him to secure a central role in planning and implementing the attack on Tarawa.

Planning for the battle of Tarawa originated with a strategy favored by Admiral Ernest J. King, who wanted to seize the offensive in 1943. Significant American victories at Midway, Attu, Gavutu, Tulagi, and Guadalcanal encouraged him to retrieve the old War Plan Orange of the 1930s, which envisioned an attack through the Marshall and Caroline Islands to reach Japan.[11] He had a difficult time convincing the Joint Chiefs and the Combined Chiefs; they finally, though begrudgingly, allowed him to launch a limited offensive in the central Pacific in 1943–1944. He was told that his victory must be logistically lean, quick, and decisive. With those strictures in mind, the Orange Plan was implemented with one major change. The original plan involved the Marshalls. But insufficient intelligence, the proximity of Japanese airfields, and the inability of American bombers to reach the Marshalls led to the selection of the Gilberts as an alternative. Betio, an island in the Tarawa atoll, was targeted because its airstrip could be used subsequently to launch aerial reconnaissance and bombing missions. The decision meant attacking a heavily fortified island surrounded by a coral reef.

King assigned Admiral Chester W. Nimitz, commander in chief of the Pacific Fleet, the task of taking Tarawa. Nimitz then designated battle-tested Vice Admiral Raymond A. Spruance to command the newly created Central Pacific Force. Nimitz and Spruance selected two principal subordinates, Rear Admiral Richmond Kelly Turner and Marine Major General Holland M. Smith. Turner would command the amphibious task forces that included all the ships and the initial assault troops. Smith would command a Marine division, an Army division, and a base defense force. Holland Smith assigned Major General Julian C. Smith, commander of the Second Marine Division, to head the assault on Betio.

General Julian Smith gathered his staff in the Windsor hotel in Wellington, New Zealand, to discuss the operation, code name GALVANIC. During these highly secret meetings, his operations officer, Lieutenant Colonel Shoup, made a suggestion that significantly influenced the outcome of the battle. While an observer at Guadalcanal, Shoup was impressed by the capabilities of the LVT (landing vehicle, tracked), or amphibian tractor ("amtrac"). Crossing the fringing coral reef under fire was extremely dangerous, Shoup noted, and these vehicles might work. Smith and his chief of staff, Colonel Merritt Edson, liked Shoup's idea and decided to investigate the possibility of converting LVTs into an assault vehicle.

LVTs were lightly armed, thin-skinned transports that could operate in water and to a limited degree on land. They often lost their tracks in soft mud, and the engine might stall in rough seas. When Smith, Edson, and Shoup met with Amphibian Tractor Battalion commander Major Henry Drewes, he cautioned against using his vehicles for combat unless they were modified substantially. They needed armor plating; more machine guns, including forward-firing .50-caliber guns; and changes to prevent stalling and throwing tracks. Even with modifications, the seventy-five LVT-1 Alligators Drewes provided were not enough for the assault. Drewes suggested that Smith ask for some of the new LVT-2 Water Buffalos available in San Diego. It was now up to Smith to convince his superiors to modify the LVTs and secure enough of them.

Julian Smith contacted his superior, General Holland Smith, to request his support for refitting the LVTs on hand and obtaining more of them. Holland Smith concurred and agreed to persuade Admiral Turner. After the aptly nicknamed "Howlin' Mad" Smith shouted at an immovable Turner, he gave him an ultimatum: "No LVT, no operation."[12] The threat worked, and fifty LVT-2s were added to those on hand. All the LVTs had to be tested to see if they were seaworthy and capable of going over reefs.

Acquiring suitable vehicles for the attack on Betio was only one of the many problems facing Julian Smith and his staff as they planned to invade a little-known island. Although they were able to amass a considerable amount of data quickly, intelligence was insufficient. A more complete picture finally emerged from aerial photography, which Shoup credited as being truly outstanding.[13] On one occasion he analyzed a photograph showing latrines. Based on a buttocks-to-latrine-hole ratio, Shoup calculated the number of Japanese soldiers on the island. After the battle his estimate proved to be remarkably accurate.[14]

Unfortunately, predicting the tides was more difficult. The coral reef surrounding Betio was a major barrier for the amphibious operation. At low tide the reef created a clear and devastating fire zone. In the upcoming battle, the tides of war literally shifted with the waves of attack. During the assault the tides remained below normal, exposing the reef, which blocked landing craft with reinforcements and supplies. Many marines had to wade ashore, a distance of eight hundred yards or more, exposed to relentless enemy fire. For American troops, the battle became a bloodbath.[15]

There were human barriers to the operation's success as well. The primary obstacle was the lack of combat experience in amphibious warfare. Julian Smith's previous command had been in training. Shoup had no combat command experience. He had been merely an observer at Guadalcanal and Rendova. The only commanders with relevant experience were Major Henry Crowe, navy Captain Herbert R. Knowles, and the hero of Guadalcanal, Colonel Edson. Julian Smith relied on Edson's experience and Shoup's insights to craft the battle plan. Edson was the principal architect, and his "Estimate of the Situation—Gilberts" (October 5, 1942) was a masterful compilation and analysis of the available intelligence. Superiors, however, undid these best-laid plans. General Holland Smith had made it clear that the Sixth Marines would be held in reserve. Consequently, the attacking force was dangerously undermanned. Conventional military wisdom dictated that attacking forces should outnumber defenders by a ratio of 3 to 1. Without the Sixth Marines, the ratio fell to 1.66 to 1. In addition, the preparatory bombardment of Betio was limited to three hours, not the several days stipulated in the Edson-Shoup plan. The final limitation was the elimination of the planned decoy landing at the adjacent island of Bairiki, which was to serve also as an artillery base.

All these limitations—too few troops, inadequate bombardment, and vetoing the Bairiki feint—infuriated Julian Smith. He appealed to Holland Smith to reverse these decisions, but the senior Smith, while sympathetic, was unyielding. Outraged, Julian Smith insisted that his orders be written, his objections noted, and that he not be held responsible for the attack under those conditions. Holland Smith obliged.

Julian Smith had good reason to be dismayed. He faced the frightful prospect of a frontal assault against one of the most heavily fortified islands in the Pacific. Smith delegated to Shoup the unenviable task of revising the battle plan and designating the landing beaches on Betio. The island resembled a bird with a long tail lying on its side, its chest facing north. Most of the Japanese defenses were on the southern coast (the bird's back) and the western coast (the bird's head). The northern beaches were not as well defended. Sticking out from the northern beach was a one-thousand-yard-long pier that looked like the bird's legs. Shoup's plan identified three landing zones on the northern beaches, each six-hundred yards long: Red Beach One encompassed the northwestern tip to the reentrance, Red Beach Two extended from the reentrance to the pier, and Red Beach Three extended from the pier eastward. Another beach, Green Beach (the bird's head) was part of a contingency plan.

Preceding the landing, a limited aerial attack and naval gunfire were designated to soften enemy defenses. Then, one regiment would land with three battalions abreast, and one regiment would be held in reserve. Before the attack, a scout sniper platoon would seize the pier. On paper, the plan was simple enough, but neither the plans nor the rehearsal could anticipate the savage fighting that occurred.

Lightly armed with his disclaimer and abridged battle plan, Smith conducted rehearsal landings at Efate until D-Day on November 20. During these exercises, he made a momentous decision. After Colonel William M. Marshall, commander of the Second Marines, suffered a

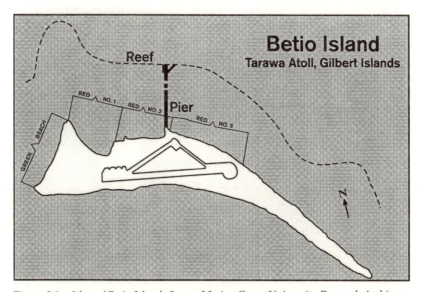

Figure 3.1. Map of Betio Island. *Source:* Marine Corps University Research Archives.

nervous breakdown,[16] Smith replaced Marshall with Shoup, immediately promoting him to colonel. Given Shoup's lack of combat command experience and the critical role the Second Marines were to play in the upcoming assault, Smith took a calculated risk. He gambled on his observation of Shoup's tough personality and keen intelligence to carry him through the battle. The gamble paid off.

On D-Day nothing went according to plan. The element of surprise quickly disappeared when Admiral Hill, commander of the Southern Attack Force, had to reposition transport vessels that were interfering with naval gunfire. The commotion alerted the Japanese, who immediately opened fire on the task force. After the initial exchange of gunfire between the Japanese shore batteries and American battleships, Admiral Hill stopped the bombardment to allow for the planned air strike. For some unknown reason the aerial attack was delayed a half hour, giving the Japanese time to regroup. After the brief hiatus, Hill ordered a resumption of naval gunfire, which continued for several hours. Then Hill ordered a cease-fire over the objections of both Smith and Edson. Without covering fire, the LVTs had to cross another four thousand yards to the beaches.

The LVTs headed for the beaches in three long waves at three-hundred-yard intervals. As Wave One advanced to the final two hundred yards to the beach, they were hit with withering firepower from the Japanese defenders. Apparently the bombardment had done little to soften the defenses. But most of the LVTs made it ashore. Later in the day, the exposed reef forced troops to wade five hundred to one thousand yards to shore under heavy enemy fire.

When the first waves of attack hit the beaches, Shoup was struggling to get to the battle. After hours of delays, he arrived at the reef about 11 A.M. As he approached the reef, he saw weaponless, retreating marines wading toward the transports. He stopped them, ordered them back to the fight, and told them to "pick up weapons from the dead and go in."[17] Shoup continued toward shore, but his journey was interrupted by heavy fire that destroyed his LVT. He finally made it to shore on his third try, slogging through the water like so many other marines on D-Day. While he was in the water, he was wounded in his legs by shell fragments and received a grazing bullet wound in his neck. Shoup sought shelter under the pier but soon realized that it offered no protection. Then he exposed himself to enemy fire, rallied troops in the water, and crouching under the pier, exhorted them: "Are there any of you cowardly sons of bitches got the guts to follow a Colonel of the Marines?"[18] They did, and he led them toward shore. Finally, just before noon he crawled on to the beach and established his command post. His headquarters was a hole in the sand behind a bunker made of thick coconut logs. It was forty feet long, eight feet wide, with two tiered walls, all completely covered with sand. Only two ventilators jutted out. Shoup ordered the ventilators to be stuffed, and he posted sentries to prevent the Japanese from escaping.[19] And from that vantage point, Shoup commanded the assault until he was relieved.

On the beach Shoup tried desperately to restore communications, secure supplies, and above all, generate momentum in the attack. His most urgent problem was communication. Most of the radios were destroyed during the initial landing waves, and Shoup had to rely on runners. Accompanying Shoup on his trek ashore was Lieutenant Colonel Evans F. Carlson, the heroic commander of the Second Raider Battalion at Makin and Guadalcanal. Carlson was an oddity in the Corps. Before World War II, he accompanied Mao Tse-Tung's communist army in China during the 1930s. He was so impressed by the morale of the communist armies, he wrote two books extolling the virtues of their *gung ho* (teamwork) philosophy. He later put this concept to use when he organized his Raider Battalion, but his superiors looked somewhat askance at this radical marine. Not Shoup. His view of Carlson was, "He may have been Red but he wasn't yellow."[20] In any event, Shoup depended on Carlson to relay firsthand information back to Admiral Hill and General Smith. Shoup told Carlson, "You tell the general and the admiral we're going to stick and fight."[21] In this way the plight of the marines became clear. Marine casualties were increasing at an alarming rate during the first day of battle, and defeat was imminent. Both commanders appealed to Admiral Turner for help, using the phrase "situation in doubt," the same words used by the losing defenders of Wake Island two years before. The ominous message was effective. Turner gave them the entire Sixth Marines, who were being held in reserve.

While Smith and Hill secured reinforcements, Shoup worked closely with Lieutenant Colonel Presley M. Rixey and his artillery battalion. Together, Shoup and Rixey decided to bring 75-mm pack howitzers ashore from landing boats stuck on the reef. Conveying these disassembled weapons ashore was a slow and arduous process that took most of the day. At night they reassembled the weapons, which were used decisively the next day.

Most of the reports Shoup received the first day were discouraging. Major Ryan's report, however, was somewhat encouraging. With a small force and two tanks, he captured more ground than anyone else. But his "victory" was modest, like all the rest. By the end of the

Figure 3.2.   Colonel Shoup holding his map case during the battle of Tarawa. *Source:* Marine Corps University Research Archives.

first day, the Marines held two toeholds totaling less than a quarter of a square mile of beach. Shoup described them as jagged as "a stock market graph." As night fell, the prospects of the marines in those small enclaves looked dim. Thirty-five hundred marines remained out of an attack force of five thousand. Those remaining huddled together, making easy targets for the Japanese. Although the Japanese were skillful night fighters, they lacked mortars. One of Shoup's staff officers, Major Rathvon McC. Tompkins, was mystified as to why the Japanese "didn't use mortars in the first night. People were lying on the beach so thick you couldn't walk."[22] For General Smith, "the night of D-Day was the greatest danger to our landing forces . . . this was the crisis of the battle."[23]

When the anticipated counterattack did not materialize, Shoup found time to confer by radio with Brigadier General Leo D. Hermle, the assistant division commander who had reached the head of the pier. He asked Hermle to have Smith land reinforcements on Red Beach Two. Hermle managed to hitch a ride out to one of the destroyers in the lagoon, where he relayed Shoup's advice on the landing zone. Fortunately, Smith concurred. If reinforcements had landed on the eastern end of the island, as originally planned, they would have been slaughtered on the heavily mined beaches.

One crisis may have passed, but another one loomed at daybreak. The marines' tenuous hold on Betio needed reinforcement. Smith ordered the First Battalion, Eighth Marines to land on Red Beach Two. From the start, everything went wrong. The tide was too low, and the landing team had to wade five hundred yards to shore facing killing Japanese fire. The early morning landing turned into a frightful bloodbath that prompted war correspondent Robert Sherrod to record: "One boat blows up, then another. The survivors start swimming ashore, but machine-gun bullets dot the water all around them."[24] For Shoup, it was the lowest point in the battle. He reported to Smith, "The situation does not look good ashore."[25]

Then, at that low point in the struggle, one extraordinarily brave man saved the day. Lieutenant William D. Hawkins of the regimental Scout and Sniper Platoon fought above and beyond the call of duty. When the attacking troops were being cut to pieces in the water, Hawkins led an attack along Red Beach Two. Out in front of his troops he charged at fortified Japanese positions, throwing grenades through their gun slits. One grenade was tossed back, wounding him severely, but he kept on going. When his unit returned to Shoup's command post, he refused medical attention and organized another attack. Once again, he was out in front of his troops. During the second attack, he was fatally wounded. Shoup observed, "It's not often that you can credit a first lieutenant with winning a battle, but Hawkins came as near as any man could."[26] For his bravery, Hawkins was awarded the Medal of Honor posthumously.

On the second day of battle, with only primitive communications, Shoup ordered the commanders of the landing teams to advance. Major Wood B. Kyle and Lieutenant Colonel Walter I. Jordan were to take the south coast. Major Henry P. Crowe and Major Robert H. Ruud on Red Beach Three were to destroy Japanese forces on their left and front. Major Michael P. Ryan without orders took all of Green Beach on the west coast. Ryan's advance proved to be the most decisive victory of the day. With the aid of a medium tank and a naval gunfire coordinator, Lieutenant Thomas Greene, he was able to direct the combined firepower of two destroyers and use the tank to cover advancing troops. Within an hour, the beach was secured. For the first time, reinforcements could land on a secure beachhead, and Ryan was in position to move eastward toward the airstrip.

In other sectors, the battle did not go as well. Marines were still being slaughtered as they tried to get ashore. Majors Crowe and Ruud were stymied on their left by large Japanese bunkers. Naval gunfire helped them, but they struggled with each step forward. Kyle and Jordan on Red Beach Two cut across to the south coast, but their hold was tenuous. Logistical problems compounded the attackers' difficulties. Shoup had to resort to stripping dead troops of their canteens, ammunition, and first aid kits.

By midafternoon, the battle shifted in favor of the attackers. Although fighting remained intense, marines had moved beyond their toeholds, and supplies of water and ammunition improved. Now Shoup could report to Smith, "Casualties: many. Percentage dead: unknown. Combat efficiency: We are winning."[27] One sign of approaching victory was the landing of the first battalion unscathed. Major William K. Jones and his troops made it to shore in rubber rafts. Dubbed "the admiral of the Condom Fleet," Jones saw little humor in his vulnerable flotilla paddling their way through mined waters. But they made it and bolstered Major Ryan's forces. By nightfall Shoup was confident of victory. He told Robert Sherrod, "Well I think we're winning, but the bastards have a lot of bullets left. I think we'll clean up tomorrow."[28] That evening General Smith sent Colonel Edson to relieve Shoup. The order gave Shoup a welcomed respite from overall command.

On the third day of battle, Edson ordered an attack on all fronts, but central to his plan was to push Major Jones's fresh troops eastward. Jones complied and, with the advantage of combined arms, moved forward. He borrowed two tanks from Major Ryan and used them in the vanguard of his assault. Each rifle company was assigned a .30-caliber machine gun to augment their firepower, and the lead company had combat engineers with flamethrowers. Jones moved forward with his heavily armed force along the south coast and connected with other American troops without suffering many casualties.

Elsewhere the fight was more savage. Major Crowe's attack was blocked by three heavily armed fortifications, including a bombproof shelter. The shelter was particularly challenging. The only way to get at the Japanese was to drop explosives into the air vents. Major William C. Chamberlain undertook the task along with First Lieutenant Alexander Bonnyman and his squad of combat engineers. They made it to the top of the mound, which apparently frightened some Japanese troops into fleeing out the rear entrance. Bonnyman's heroic effort inspired the rest of the marines to destroy the rear entrance and kill hundreds of fleeing Japanese. Bonnyman's heroism was later recognized with a posthumous award of the Medal of Honor.

On Red Beaches One and Two the Japanese were still in control. General Smith landed on Green Beach about noon. When he tried to lead his group to a landing craft and make for the center of the island, he was almost killed. He did not reach the Edson-Shoup command post until 3:00 p.m. From that vantage point Smith learned of the dramatic successes of the marines. But overall, progress was slow and casualties were high. He informed the flagship that it might take five more days to defeat the Japanese.

That evening, Smith assumed overall command of the operation on the island. His seven thousand marines greatly outnumbered the Japanese, but he believed he would need more reinforcements to flush out the remaining Japanese and resist any counterattacks. Actually, the counterattacks that occurred on the third and fourth days worked to his advantage. The Japanese lost so many troops in their attacks that American troops far outnumbered the remaining defenders. During the third night, Major Jones and his men repulsed four attacks without any reinforcements.

Counterattacks continued on the fourth day. But Smith was able to report to Admiral Hill, "Decisive defeat of enemy counterattack last night destroyed bulk of hostile resistance. Expect complete annihilation of enemy on Betio this date."[29] Still, there was more fighting to be done, particularly on the borders of Red Beaches One and Two. There Shoup was in command, trying to subdue the Japanese at the "re-entrant" (bird's neck) where so many marines had lost their lives. He directed Majors Hay and Schoettel to encircle the Japanese, which they did by late afternoon. All resistance ceased.

Shoup reported victory to Smith. The final objectives on Betio were taken. The battle was over. For three and a half days Marines and Japanese had been locked in a savage, often hand-to-hand, struggle. Almost 5,000 Japanese had been killed. American casualties totaled 3,407, of which one-third were deaths. Up to that time, it was the bloodiest engagement in the Pacific.

When reports of the costly victory reached the United States, a triumph was viewed as a tragedy. Newspaper headlines announced a terrible waste of life.[30] Even military leaders questioned the wisdom of the attack. General MacArthur, for example, observed, "These frontal assaults by the Navy, as at Tarawa, are a tragic and unnecessary massacre of human lives."[31] President Roosevelt was shocked too. When he saw Robert Sherrod at a news conference, he asked him for guidance. Having just returned from the battle, Sherrod thought the painful truth about war must be told. He suggested that Roosevelt release the films of the battle.

Roosevelt did, and the documentary *With the Marines at Tarawa* was a stunning success.[32]

To further bring home the realities of war, Colonel Edson was summoned to the United States. He answered the critics, cautioning, "I think the American people should realize the psychology of the people we are fighting—to make the campaigns as costly as possible because they don't believe we can take it."[33] The reality of the price of victory in the Pacific was now known.

Controversy over Tarawa raged at the time and for many years. General Holland Smith revived the criticism in his memoir *Coral and Brass*. Five years after the battle, in 1948, he wrote that it was "a terrible waste of life and effort"[34] and Tarawa should have been bypassed. Some found his retrospective judgment disingenuous. General Julian Smith rejoined, "I do not recall that General H. M. Smith offered any objection to moving against Tarawa"[35] at the time of the battle. Everyone else in command at Tarawa thought it was worth the fight, including Nimitz, Spruance, Edson, and Shoup. It proved the viability of amphibious warfare and provided valuable lessons for future attacks.

For Shoup, the battle was his finest hour. He helped plan and later fought in the attack. He held the assault together during the first critical day and a half. To his comrades in arms there, he was "a Marine's Marine."[36] With scant experience before Tarawa, he learned quickly while fighting. General Jones recalls, "He was superb. Very cool. Recognized exactly a situation, read it soundly, militarily. Didn't allow his emotions to come into the decision making process at all. He would judge and accept the casualties that he knew that this course of action was going to require. And he always tried to do it with losing the fewest Marines. I'd say he's a very fine, cool, competent combat commander."[37]

Shoup's bravery at Tarawa earned him the Medal of Honor. Julian Smith wrote in his recommendation that when troops took cover and clung to the pier, Shoup got them started again. He wrote, "After all else had failed to get the men moving Colonel Shoup, at the risk of his life, stepped into the open and called to the men to follow him. Because of his example the men took courage and followed him to the beach where they took their place in the fight."[38]

Tarawa left an indelible impression on Shoup. On the last day of battle he wrote a short verse.

> Drag from my sight this
> Blear-eyed
> Thing
> That was my friend

Return all to Mother Earth
Except
That ring
To prove his end
On Tarawa[39]

Long after the battle, Shoup remembered the terrible cost of victory. Ten years later, he wrote that "there was never any doubt in the minds of those ashore as to what the final outcome of the battle for Tarawa would be. There was for some seventy-six hours, however, considerable haggling with the enemy over the exact price we were to pay. It was during this period of bargaining that the world, foe and friend alike, had demonstrated to them the extraordinary willingness and the immeasurable capability of the American fighting man to defeat the best of the Japanese armed forces."[40] At an even later date, on the twenty-fifth anniversary of the battle in 1968, Shoup returned to Betio to dedicate a memorial pylon cenotaph. He honored all those who had died there, Americans and Japanese, and ended with a prayer: "Please, God, may our ships of state sail on and on in a world forever at peace."[41]

After Tarawa, Shoup served as chief of staff of the Second Marine Division during the Saipan and Tinian campaigns in the Mariana Islands. Admiral King justified the strategy of leaping one thousand miles from the Marshalls to the Marianas because the large islands in the Marianas—Saipan, Tinian, and Guam—would be bases for attacks against Luzon, Formosa, and the Japanese home islands. While Shoup's role in these operations was not as dramatic or central as his leadership at Tarawa, he continued to perform courageously. General Wallace M. Greene Jr. recalled how he and Shoup were stranded in a forward observer position during a Japanese tank attack on Saipan. With only two weapons between them, a .45-caliber pistol and a bayonet, Shoup remained calm. Greene marveled at Shoup's equanimity in combat.[42] Shoup never appeared afraid of anything. For his work during these campaigns, Shoup was recognized with a second Legion of Merit with Combat "V." Soon after these operations, in October 1944, Shoup returned to the United States, a hero who never forgot the cost of victory.

Notes

1. Mrs. Zola Shoup, interview with the author, November 11, 1985.
2. David M. Shoup to Zola Shoup, Iceland, December 17, 1941.
3. David M. Shoup to Zola Shoup, Iceland, December 27, 1941.
4. Carey A. Randall, interview with the author, June 3, 1987.

5. David M. Shoup, *Officer Fitness Report*—U.S. Marine Corps, August 25, 1926.

6. Shoup, *Officer Fitness Report*, passim.

7. William K. Jones, interview with the author, February 17, 1987.

8. Jones interview.

9. Jones interview.

10. F. Paul Henderson, interview with the author, February 14, 1987.

11. See Allan R. Millett, *Semper Fidelis: The History of the United States Marine Corps* (New York, 1980), 393–99.

12. Quoted in Joseph H. Alexander, *Utmost Savagery: The Three Days of Tarawa* (Annapolis, Md., 1995), 60.

13. Alexander, *Utmost Savagery*, 70.

14. Dino Brugioni, "Tarawa–A New Prospective," *Leatherneck*, 66, no. 10 (November 1983): 38.

15. Alexander, *Utmost Savagery*, passim.

16. Alexander, *Utmost Savagery*, 94.

17. Alexander, *Utmost Savagery*, 121.

18. Alexander, *Utmost Savagery*, 137.

19. Robert Sherrod, *Tarawa: The Story of a Battle* (New York, 1944), 198.

20. Martin Russ, *Line of Departure: Tarawa* (Garden City, N.Y., 1975), 44.

21. Alexander, *Utmost Savagery*, 9.

22. Alexander, *Utmost Savagery*, 143.

23. Alexander, *Utmost Savagery*, 147.

24. Alexander, *Utmost Savagery*, 162

25. Alexander, *Utmost Savagery*, 164

26. Alexander, *Utmost Savagery*, 167.

27. Joseph H. Alexander, *Across the Reef: The Marine Assault of Tarawa* (Washington, D.C., 1993), 33.

28. Alexander, *Across the Reef*, 34.

29. Alexander, *Across the Reef*, 43.

30. Alexander, *Utmost Savagery*, 227–28.

31. Alexander, *Utmost Savagery*, 229.

32. Alexander, *Utmost Savagery*.

33. Alexander, *Utmost Savagery*, 231.

34. Alexander, *Utmost Savagery*, 243. See also Smith and Finch, *Coral and Brass*, 134.

35. Quoted in Alexander, *Utmost Savagery*, 243.

36. Alexander, *Utmost Savagery*, 48.

37. Jones interview.

38. Shoup, *Officer Fitness Report*, May 27, 1944.

39. Shoup, David M., MS Collection, Hoover Institution.

40. Sherrod, *Tarawa*, 198.

41. Sherrod, *Tarawa*, 156.

42. Wallace M. Greene Jr. interview with the author, February 23, 1981.

4

Line of Departure

From 1944 to 1959, Shoup served in a variety of assignments that helped prepare him for his future role as commandant of the Marine Corps. It was also a time when the existence of the Corps as a major combat arm of the military was threatened. While Shoup did not participate in the Corps's struggle for its right to fight, he benefited from the casualties of that battle. He was selected to be commandant by a secretary of the Navy who despised the Marine Corps officers who campaigned against reorganization of the services. Many of those officers were senior to Shoup and more likely candidates to be commandant, and Shoup's selection sent a clear message to the rebels. It was not, however, just a vendetta. The Corps needed to be reformed, and Shoup was the right man for the job. In many ways, the decade and a half following World War II was a line of departure for Shoup and the Corps as they marshalled their forces against internal and external enemies.

The external threat occurred first. While the Pacific war was still raging, several marine officers learned that the Corps might have to defend its mission in the armed services. General Victor H. Krulak remembers three episodes in 1942 and 1943 that signaled trouble. In October 1942, he was part of a team invited to instruct the Army's Twenty-fifth Infantry Division in amphibious warfare. As he was preparing to leave this assignment, General J. Lawton Collins told them that the Army would overcome its deficiencies in amphibious warfare and would end its dependency on the Marine Corps for advice.[1]

Shortly after Krulak's team finished instructing the Twenty-fifth Division, another incident revealed the Army's hostility to the Marine Corps. In December 1942, Marine Major General Alexander A. Vandegrift stopped at Nouméa,

New Caledonia, on his way to Australia to pay his respects to Admiral Halsey. With him was Lieutenant Colonel Merrill B. Twining, his operations officer. Twining met his brother there, Army Air Force Brigadier General Nathan F. Twining. One evening after a dinner party that included several high-ranking officers, some good-natured interservice banter turned ugly. At one point, Nathan Twining attacked the way the Navy and Marines had handled the battle at Guadalcanal, and he went on to say that organizational changes were underway to prevent any future Navy-Marine incursions into the domain of other military branches. Twining's diatribe was supported by a fellow Army officer, Major General J. Lawton Collins, who later figured prominently in the postwar military reorganization controversy. In any case, Merrill Twining was so disturbed by the comments of these Army officers that he reported the conversation to General Vandegrift. Vandegrift dismissed the whole affair as just interservice rivalry.[2]

A far more serious episode took place a year later. General George C. Marshall, Army Chief of Staff, submitted a memorandum to the Joint Chiefs of Staff presenting his views on reorganization of the services. He envisioned a unified defense department that included a separate air force, a single chief of staff, and a general to supervise the armed forces. No provision was made for the Marine Corps in his plan. To some officers, such as Admiral Claude C. Bloch, president of the Navy General Board, it was an outrageous scheme.[3]

Marshall's reorganization plan later surfaced in Congress when Representative James Wadsworth introduced a resolution, in March 1944, to create a Select Committee on Post War Military Policy. Soon after the committee was created, Army Lieutenant General Joseph McNarney presented it with a variation of Marshall's recommendation. McNarney's arrangement called for an independent air force and a military service chief who could bypass the secretary of defense and advise the president on strategic and budgetary matters. Again, the Marine Corps was omitted. The committee concluded, in June 1944, that the services should consider reorganization.

The Joint Chiefs responded to the challenge by forming a committee of Army and Navy officers under the direction of Admiral James O. Richardson to investigate reorganization. After interviewing eighty officers, the majority of the committee concluded that a plan similar to Marshall's would work. Richardson dissented and signaled potential interservice rivalry. When the Joint Chiefs received the report, a lively debate ensued along Army-Navy lines. Given the divergent views, it was decided to bury the report. It resurfaced when Secretary of the Navy James V. Forrestal heard about it and decided to approach President Truman. To Forrestal's dismay, he found the president sympathetic to Marshall's view of reorganization. Forrestal then decided to conduct his own inquiry and enlisted investment banker Ferdinand Eberstadt to study reorganization. Eberstadt's investigation led to an entirely different approach than Marshall's. He saw the need for an overall commander of the armed forces, and he argued for keeping the Joint Chiefs of Staff. He also suggested that three cabinet-level departments—War, Navy, and Army—report directly to the president.

Therefore by 1945, before the war ended, it was clear that an interservice conflict was brewing. On one side, the Army embraced Marshall's proposal for a single department of defense led by a civilian secretary and an overall chief of the armed forces. Together, the secretary and the chief would determine budget and missions for the services. The Joint Chiefs of Staff would continue to function but only as an advisory group. The Army Air Force would become a separate service with a mission in strategic bombing and base assignments. On the other side of the battle line stood Secretary Forrestal, who endorsed Eberstadt's recommendations that provided for greater civilian–military interaction and the preservation of the Joint Chiefs as a substantive body.[4]

While the reorganization maneuvering was taking place, the Marine Corps was either ignored or diminished in the deliberations. Understandably, the new Marine commandant in 1944, Lieutenant General Alexander A. Vandegrift, took matters into his own hands. He ordered Lieutenant Colonel Merrill Twining, under the direction of Brigadier General Gerald C. Thomas, to form a Marine Corps Board to study amphibious doctrine and to plan for the Corps's future. In effect, Twining was to be the point man in the 1945–1947 skirmishes against reorganizational threats to the Corps.

Surrounding Twining were a number of Marine officers who often worked informally with one another and without close supervision. They faced a difficult campaign on the fields of congressional lobbying and public relations. Few of the officers had the skills or experience to fight in that arena. But with Twining and his able assistant, Victor Krulak, doing much of the grunt work and others contributing their various skills, they performed effectively. They dubbed themselves the Little Men's Chowder and Marching Society, after a group in the comic strip *Barnaby*, and their formulations "chowder," a dish that some politicians found hard to swallow.

Some marines also found their stew hard to ingest. At that time, Twining and Krulak were at the Marine Corps Educational Center in Quantico, Virginia, to study amphibious warfare under the direction of Brigadier General Oliver P. Smith. They spent much of their time preparing documents to alert Congress and the public to the dangers of reorganization legislation. Smith did not appreciate their extracurricular activity, which he described as "wheels within wheels."[5] Often Twining had to ask General Thomas to help him persuade Smith that he and Krulak were not just wheeling and wheedling for the Corps. They were not. They believed that civilian control over the military was in jeopardy and that the Corps needed legislative protection as well.

Their first opportunity came in October 1945. Colonel Twining wrote a speech for General Vandegrift to be delivered to the Senate Military Affairs Committee. The speech contended that the Army's reorganization plan would allow the military to intrude upon the civilian domain and would reduce congressional control over the military. Furthermore, the proposed supreme military commander would have too much power. Vandegrift found little support from fellow officers. Army officers who testified denigrated the Corps. Even naval officers, with one notable exception, were not much help. Only Admiral Halsey praised the Corps.[6]

Others, including President Truman, were less enthusiastic about the Corps's future. In December 1945, Truman asked Congress to consider reorganization of the military. He endorsed the War Department's proposal to have a single chief of staff. While he publicly acknowledged the need for the Corps, privately he deprecated Marines as the Navy's "own little Army that talks Navy."[7]

More bad news was on its way in December 1945. Brigadier General Merritt A. Edson met with Twining and Krulak at General Thomas's behest. Edson was the Marine Corps representative in the Office of the Chief of Naval Operations and was privy to information of particular interest to the Corps. Edson shared with Twining and Krulak a report he had received from the Joint Strategy Survey Committee, an advisory group that reported to the Joint Chiefs of Staff. The document, "Missions of the Land, Sea and Air Forces," stated that it was the responsibility of the Navy Department to maintain the Marine Corps for minor operations and garrison duties. They all knew that doomed the Corps, but they could not use the document to combat reorganization because it was part of the "JCS 1478 Series," labeled top secret. Therefore its contents could not be revealed to Congress or the public.

Protected by the cloak of secrecy in the 1478 Series, some officers spoke candidly. In JCS 1478/10 and 1478/11, two Army generals took aim at the Marine Corps. General Carl Spaatz stated bluntly that he believed that Marine amphibious operations intruded into the Army and Air Force domains.[8] General Eisenhower, the army chief of staff, wanted the Corps reduced in size. He maintained that Marine units should be small, lightly armed, and never expanded during wartime.[9] To marines reading these statements in the 1478 Series, there could be no doubt about the Army's intentions. The trials that lay ahead for the Marine Corps began when General Vandegrift was summoned to appear before the Senate Naval Affairs Committee on May 10, 1946. His speech, prepared by Twining and Krulak, held nothing back. Vandegrift told the committee that "this bill 9S.2044 gives the War Department a free hand in accomplishing its expressed desire to reduce the Marine Corps to a position of military insignificance. . . . The Marine Corps thus believes it has earned this right—to have its future decided by the legislative body which created it—nothing more. . . . The bended knee is not a tradition of our Corps. If the Marine as a fighting man has not made a case for himself after 170 years, he must go. But I think you will agree with me that he has earned the right to depart with dignity and honor, not by subjugation to the status of uselessness and servility planned for him by the War Department."[10]

Vandegrift's "bended knee" speech persuaded the leaders of the Senate and House naval committees to abandon the bill. But the battle was not over. In late 1946 and early 1947, President Truman ordered Secretary of the Navy James V. Forrestal and Secretary of the Army Robert P. Patterson to reconcile the Army and Navy differences over reorganization. What emerged from their efforts was a joint statement that, in many ways, was a Navy capitulation. Most disturbing from the Marine Corps point of view was the absence of any indication of the missions of the respective services. The responsibilities of the services were to be determined later by executive order.

This turn of events troubled Vandegrift, who immediately recognized the implications of the secretarial compromise. He anticipated more struggles to persuade Congress and decided to organize a group he called the Board to Conduct Research and Prepare Material in Connection with Pending Legislation. The name described its function, but it came to be known as the Edson-Thomas board for its leaders, Brigadier Generals Edson and Gerald C. Thomas. The generals enlisted Colonel Twining, Lieutenant Colonel Krulak, and other members of the Chowder Society. Together, the members of the board set out to protect the Marine Corps in any unification of the services and to maintain civilian control by retaining the service secretaries and eliminating the proposed single chief of staff.

On February 26, 1946, the compromise proposal of the secretaries, with endorsements from Admiral Forrest Sherman, the chief of naval operations, and Army Air Force General Lauris Norstad, was presented to the Senate Armed Services Committee. The Marines feared the committee would sympathize with the Army's point of view, and Vandegrift's appearance before the committee did not help their cause. Ultimately, he agreed to a very tepid statement about the Corps's position in the reorganization scheme. Consequently, the committee supported the secretarial compromise with little alteration, and the Senate approved the bill on July 9.

The battle then shifted to the House, where the bill was referred to the Committee on Expenditures in the Executive Department. The Marines welcomed the referral because Congressman Clare E. Hoffman, who chaired the committee, was sympathetic to the Corps. Hoffman knew the father of one of the members of the Chowder Society, Lieutenant Colonel James D. Hittle. Hittle, with Twining's help, used his family connection to win over Hoffman to the Marine point of view. Additional persuasion came in the form of lobbying by the Veterans of Foreign Wars (VFW). One strategically placed member of the VFW, John Williamson, a first lieutenant in the Marine Corps Reserve, was an assistant to Omar Ketchum, the national legislative representative of the VFW. Williamson used his position to channel questions to the committee, questions prepared by the Chowder Society that exposed the dangers to the Corps in the proposed legislation. Hoffman used the questions to convince the committee to accept amendments to the bill that also had been prepared by the Chowder Society. But the most effective maneuver was Hoffman's success in getting the 1478 Series top-secret reports to the committee. That information left no doubt as to the Army's intentions.

Marine Corps lobbying annoyed President Truman. He told Vandegrift to "get those Lieutenant Colonels off the Hill and keep them off."[11] Vandegrift promptly dissolved the Edson-Thomas board, but that did not silence Edson. He retired so that he could address the Hoffman committee as a private citizen. In that capacity, he presented them with a proposal that had been designed by the board. Hoffman appropriated the Edson draft and steered it through his committee, the House, and finally the joint House-Senate conference committee. Hoffman prevailed. The conference committee accepted most of Hoffman's recommendations, including a clear statement of the Marine Corps's mission. Both the House and the Senate moved quickly and approved the bill. Truman signed the National Security Act on July 25, 1947.

The National Security Act marked a significant achievement for the Marine Corps but not total victory. Under the new law, the Corps could still be deprived of resources and lacked a voice in strategic planning. To remedy the situation, more congressional action was needed. Fortunately, sympathetic legislators such as Senator Paul Douglas and Congressmen Carl Vinson and Mike Mansfield supported the Corps by sponsoring legislation to make the commandant a member of the Joint Chiefs of Staff. Their effort culminated in Public Law 416, signed by Truman on June 20, 1952, which provided for the commandant's participation on the Joint Chiefs of Staff when their deliberations affected the Corps. In practice, the Marines were rarely excluded. At the end of the first year, only 9 percent of the Joint Chiefs' agenda items were inapplicable. Equally important, the legislation stipulated that the Corps would maintain three combat divisions and three aircraft wings.

Challenges to the Marines continued when Eisenhower became president in 1953. Not long after he was elected, Eisenhower authorized two studies of military organization, ostensibly to explore ways of avoiding interservice rivalry and overlapping functions. Later, in 1958, he asked Congress to consider increasing the power of the Secretary of Defense to include, among other prerogatives, the authority to abolish or reassign the combat functions of the armed services. Once again it appeared that the Corps might be deprived of its mission. Commandant Randolph McCall Pate responded, urging the House Armed Services Committee to continue legislative guarantees for Marine Corps functions. It was to no avail. In the end, Eisenhower got much of what he wanted.

The 1958 legislation did not undermine the Corps. By that time the Marine Corps's position in the military structure was protected by the National Security Act, enhanced by the commandant's new role on the Joint Chiefs of Staff and a 1954 General Order No. 5 that made the commandant responsible to the secretary of the Navy for overall performance of the Corps. In many ways, the reorganization struggle was the line of departure for the modern Marine Corps, which was now poised for a brighter future with a different administration in 1961.

Shoup was not involved in the merger fight. His line of departure was to be a rendezvous with fiscal bureaucracy and recruit training. None of this was immediately apparent after World War II. His initial assignments were routine. He first served in the Plans and Policies Division at Headquarters for two years. Then he had a service command with the Fleet Marine Force at Pearl Harbor combined with occasional duty on the Marine Corps Board and Marine Corps schools. A year later, he was transferred to Quantico, where he commanded the Basic

School from 1950 to 1952. His next assignment was back at Headquarters, where he was to help modernize the Corps's budgetary, fiscal, and supply problems. There he met the goliath of the Corps's bureaucrats, General William P. T. Hill.[12]

General Hill's domination of the supply and financial operations of the Marine Corps was legendary. He had capitalized on the merger of the quartermaster and paymaster functions into a single Supply Department and created a seemingly unassailable empire. Tough and smart, Hill became the darling of the congressional appropriations committees. His theatrical presentations before Congress included such props as a small green memo pad he kept in his back pocket. When questioned he would recite from memory the most minute details of the Corps budget. Or he might read from his memo pad citing how little the Marines paid for an item compared with the Army. But fellow marines were not enamored of his behavior. He resisted change and even frustrated the reform efforts of some commandants, such as General Clifton B. Cates. With powerful friends in Congress, Hill was not to be trifled with.

Still, reform could not be avoided. The budget cuts during the Eisenhower administration and the president's insistence on streamlining the process compelled a new commandant in 1952, General Lemuel C. Shepherd, to reorganize the Corps's financial operations. Ultimately, he adopted a plan designed by Krulak that separated supply from a newly created office of fiscal director, which would handle budgeting and accounting. Shepherd selected the recently promoted Brigadier General Shoup to head the new division. That assignment involved the unenviable task of wresting control from General Hill. Shoup was the appropriate choice because no one could intimidate him. General Gerald C. Thomas remembered:

> Hill fought him at every step, and Hill's a fighter. He's got a lot of Indian in him. He's part Comanche Indian. Shoup had a real rough time, and he used to come up and Brute Krulak and I would salve his wounds and he'd go back again. But it took two years to do that job. But he stayed with it. And I don't think I could put my hand on another officer in the Marine Corps that would have been sturdy enough to have swung that job like Shoup did. . . . Stubborn enough. Mean. Mean as hell. He did the job. They had many battles and they went in to Shepherd many, many times, but each time Shepherd would finally vote for Shoup. They fought all the details out, one by one by one, over a period of two years. Terrific. But we needed that. The Marine Corps needed it. Not only did we need it but we were in trouble over at the Pentagon. And the Navy Department. Because we didn't have a fiscal setup that functioned with them.[13]

By the end of his assignment, Hill was so pleased with Shoup's energy and intelligence that he wrote glowing fitness reports. From the outset, Hill found that Shoup "approached the job with zeal and confidence" and was "outstanding in all respects."[14] Shepherd agreed, and after Hill retired, he recommended Shoup's promotion to major general.

Shoup's success in fiscal reorganization earned him a reputation for troubleshooting, and he was soon given another tough assignment. Shortly after the new commandant, General Randolph McCall Pate, took command in 1956, a tragic accident occurred at the Recruit Depot on Parris Island. On April 8, drill instructor (DI) Staff Sergeant Matthew C. McKeon led his platoon of recruits on a punishment march in a river behind the rifle range. Six of them drowned.

From the outset, the Ribbon Creek incident was a media event. When reporters learned that the drill instructor had been drinking before the march, they knew they had front-page copy. Pate tried unsuccessfully to control the media assault on the Corps's reputation. In desperation he went to Parris Island to assure reporters that any DI guilty of abuse would be punished. But the press barrage continued.

Pate was more successful in shielding the Corps from a congressional inquisition. He appealed to sympathetic members of the House to block an investigation and give the Marines a chance to clean up their own mess. With that danger behind him, Pate immediately convened a court of inquiry, which, like a grand jury, would determine if prosecution was warranted. He assigned Brigadier General Wallace M. Greene Jr. to head the panel. At the same time, he appointed two generals to head independent Recruit Training commands, one for San Diego, the other for Parris Island. Greene assumed command at Parris Island and Brigadier General Alan Shapley took command of the San Diego depot. Both generals were to report to the commandant through a newly created Inspector General of Recruit Training. Shoup received that assignment.

These organizational changes were not as urgent as the McKeon inquiry, and consequently General Greene and his court of inquiry moved swiftly. On April 20, 1956, they reported their findings, which included a formal charge recommending that the sergeant be tried by general court-martial. He was cited for four violations of the Uniform Code of Military Justice: using alcoholic beverages in a barracks; oppressing recruits; drinking in front of recruits; and the most serious charge, negligent and oppressive manslaughter.

On July 16, the trial started and moved quickly to conclusion. A brilliant New York attorney, Emile Zola Berman, represented McKeon.

He defended his client by pointing to McKeon's service record and exemplary personal life. In the end, however, Berman managed to convince the court only that the deaths were not intentional. When the court reached its verdict on August 4, it found McKeon guilty of negligent homicide and drinking on duty. He was sentenced to reduction in rank to private, a fine, incarceration for nine months, and a bad conduct discharge. To many Corps loyalists the punishment seemed too harsh, and they lobbied the Secretary of the Navy to reduce the sentence. Thomas agreed, probably to avoid any more adverse publicity.

The case was not closed for the Corps. Its tarnished reputation needed to be cleared, a process that started even before McKeon's trial. After Greene finished his work with the court of inquiry, he learned on May 1 that he had been named commanding general of Recruit Training at Parris Island with virtually a free hand to rebuild the depot. On May 7, Greene telephoned Shoup, indicating his plans and listing his needs. Shoup followed up the conversation with a personal meeting the next day. Their exchange was cordial. In many ways it was a reunion of comrades in arms. They had served together in China in the 1930s and had shared a foxhole on Saipan during a Japanese counterattack. At their conference, Shoup stressed the importance of keeping basic training tough.[15] He also told Greene that Headquarters planned to send thousands of questionnaires to bases to learn what marines thought about their basic training.

Shoup returned to Washington immediately, but he remained in close contact with Greene and the base. Earlier, he had sent members of his staff to interview drill instructors. From these interviews and Greene's reports, Shoup learned that the DIs wanted better housing, more uniforms, and free laundry. Shoup's primary contribution was helping Greene meet these needs, but Headquarters was not always generous, and it took Shoup's heavy hand to get the job done. Many senior officers were annoyed with Shoup, but Greene was grateful.[16]

The Greene-Shoup team was effective. As a result of their efforts, more officers were assigned to the depot, screening and training of DIs was intensified, and their living conditions improved. Physical conditioning for recruits was strengthened, and everyone's morale was elevated. One change symbolized their accomplishments. The old wide-brimmed field hats of pre–World War II days were reintroduced. It became emblematic of the tough DI.

Shoup's tour as Inspector General of Recruit Training ended in 1957, when he became Inspector General for the Corps. Under his guidance, substantial reforms in recruit training had occurred. But that was to change suddenly. Without the fresh glare of Ribbon Creek publicity and Shoup's driving will, training reform stalled. Greene's fortunes changed too. He committed a series of public relations blunders that embroiled him in controversy with the press. Without a protector like Shoup to help him, his career seemed to unravel. He was passed over for promotion to major general, and it looked as if his career was finished. But that all changed when Shoup became commandant and their partnership was restored.

Notes

1. Victor H. Krulak, *First to Fight: An Inside View of the U.S. Marine Corps* (Annapolis, Md., 1984), 17–18.

2. Krulak, *First to Fight*, 18.

3. Krulak, *First to Fight*, 19.

4. See Edwin H. Simmons, "The Marines: Survival and Accommodation," address to the George C. Marshall Foundation Conference, Lexington, Virginia, March 25–26, 1977. Gordon W. Keiser, *The Marine Corps and Defense Unification, 1944–47: The Politics of Survival* (Washington, D.C., 1982). Thomas Gates, interview with the author, May 26, 1982; Krulak, *First to Fight*, 24. See also Enthoven and Smith, *How Much Is Enough?* chapter 2. Wallace M. Greene interview with the author, February 23, 1981.

5. Krulak, *First to Fight*, 29.

6. Krulak, *First to Fight*, 30.

7. Krulak, *First to Fight*, 31.

8. Krulak, *First to Fight*, 34.

9. Krulak, *First to Fight*, 34.

10. U.S. Congress, Senate, Committee on Naval Affairs, Hearings on S 2044, 79th Congress, 2d Session, (Washington, D.C., 1946), 118–19.

11. Krulak, *First to Fight*, 39.

12. Lemuel C. Shepherd Jr., Oral History Transcript, Headquarters Marine Corps, Historical Division, 1967, 480.

13. Oral History Transcript, General Gerald C. Thomas, History and Museum Divisions, Oral History Collection, H.Q.M.C., 920–21.

14. David M. Shoup Fitness Report.

15. Keith Fleming, *The U.S. Marine Corps in Crisis: Ribbon Creek and Recruit Training* (Columbia, S.C., 1990), 62.

16. Greene interview.

5

"Crackpot Realism"

Shoup took command of the Marine Corps in 1960, the last year of the Eisenhower administration. By that time Eisenhower's New Look defense policy was firmly entrenched, and he had established a record of both successes and failures. In many ways, there was nothing new in the Eisenhower approach to national security. He accepted Truman's containment doctrine, but he wanted to block communist expansion without any increase in government spending. Achieving that goal required limiting conventional military power and weapons development and, alternatively, relying on the threat of "massive retaliation" and "brinkmanship," journalistic labels for the reliance on thermonuclear weapons, air power, and the threat of unlimited war. The administration's approach seemed to work. There were no wars and communist expansion was held in check.[1] But Eisenhower's New Look overlooked the implications of rising nationalism in Africa and Asia, ignored reformist zeal in Cuba and Guatemala, and proved ineffective in pacifying the Middle East. Furthermore, reliance on covert operations in places like Iran and Guatemala and support for a disreputable government in South Vietnam bequeathed a legacy of foreign distrust and armed conflict to future administrations.

Justifiably, in one instance Eisenhower could claim that he offered a new and effective alternative to Truman's Asian policy. When the Korean conflict changed from a war of containment to a crusade for unification, it failed. Eisenhower had inherited a military stalemate and diplomatic impasse. But in this situation, his promise to continue negotiations along with the threat of nuclear attack helped to end the war in 1953.

In other parts of Asia, Eisenhower's strategy was less successful. Massive retaliation and brinkmanship could not be applied to Indochina, where he continued Truman's policy of aiding the French in their effort to suppress a colonial uprising. Both presidents viewed the overthrow of French rule as the prelude to further attempts to dislodge colonial rulers and invite communist infiltration, the so-called domino effect. But Eisenhower was reluctant to help the French, who he thought were bungling the war. Consequently, when a substantial French force was besieged at Dien Bien Phu in 1954, he refused to intervene without the support of the British and Congress. Neither was forthcoming, and the French were left to their fate.

A new French government under Pierre Mendès-France accepted defeat and agreed to negotiate with the insurgents (the Vietminh) and the British, Chinese, and Soviets in Geneva. The United States did not participate but agreed to support the Geneva accords that divided the country temporarily at the seventeenth parallel pending a general election under United Nations supervision to create a unified government. In the meantime, the United States sent aid to the government of South Vietnam during the fall of 1954, and increased support when the French departed. Apparently, fear that general elections would place the communist Ho Chi Minh in power encouraged the administration to continue aiding South Vietnam after agreeing with the latter's decision to block the 1956 elections. The policy of keeping Vietnam divided while further buttressing the south continued between 1956 and 1960, and included American military aid to establish the army of the Republic of South Vietnam. Eisenhower was thus setting the stage for greater and ultimately disastrous commitments to South Vietnam by future presidents.

Eisenhower's defense policy in Asia also involved reassessing American policy toward China. Republicans charged during the 1952 campaign that the Truman administration was not supporting the nationalists in Taiwan in their attempt to retake their homeland, which had fallen to the communists in 1949. Talk of unleashing Jiang Jieshi to attack the mainland, which emerged during the Korean War, persisted when Eisenhower took office. At the very least, the new president was determined to protect the exiled Chinese.[2] When Zhou Enlai, the Chinese Communist foreign minister, threatened to take Taiwan from the Nationalists in 1954, Eisenhower sent the Seventh Fleet to protect the island. Subsequently he sent Secretary of State John Foster Dulles to negotiate a defense treaty with the Nationalists that guaranteed the defense of Taiwan. Nothing was said about other islands, namely, Quemoy and Matsu, which both the nationalists and the communists claimed.

The situation in Taiwan worsened in 1955, when the communists attacked the Tachen Islands in January. Located about two hundred miles northwest of Taiwan, they were of no vital interest to the Nationalists, and Eisenhower helped in the evacuation of Nationalist troops located at this remote outpost. He used the occasion to ask Congress for the authority to use force to protect Taiwan and the Pescadores chain. Quemoy and Matsu were not mentioned.

In February 1955, when Secretary of State Dulles returned from his trip to Asia, he expressed alarm at the seriousness of the Taiwan situation.[3] A month later, he told reporters that a communist attack on Quemoy or Matsu would foreshadow an invasion of Taiwan, and he raised the specter of using atomic weapons to defend the nationalists. Eisenhower agreed and indicated he saw no reason why tactical nuclear weapons could not be used if a conflict arose. All the talk of war and of the use of nuclear weapons generated widespread anxiety, and some Democrats expressed their opposition to a war over two insignificant islands. But Eisenhower's threat was vague. It was a warning, not an ultimatum. Fortunately, nothing happened, and the United States moved away from the brink of nuclear war.

Eisenhower used a more subtle approach elsewhere. When nationalist uprisings appeared to threaten American interests in developing countries, he authorized the CIA to sponsor covert operations to bring about regime changes. Two notable examples of cloak-and-dagger warfare occurred in Iran in 1953 and Guatemala in 1954. In Iran, the administration responded to the politics of oil in the Middle East.[4] When Iran Prime Minister Mohammed Mossadeq nationalized the Anglo-Iranian oil company, American companies joined the international boycott of Iranian oil. Mossadeq responded by informing Eisenhower that he would be forced to seek Soviet aid. Publicly, Eisenhower encouraged negotiation with the British; privately, he planned to overthrow the Iranian government. He ordered the CIA to engineer a coup and make the figurehead Shah, Mohammed Reza Pahlevi, the effective ruler of Iran. World War II spy veteran Kermit Roosevelt was selected to lead the CIA operation, which was launched in early August. Within a month, Roosevelt recruited a bizarre assortment of pro-shah revolutionists—athletes, entertainers, and slum dwellers—who placed the shah in power with American help in September. Eisenhower congratulated the shah and immediately offered financial assistance.

On the other side of the globe, in Central America, Eisenhower's fear that a nationalist uprising might turn communist led to another secret operation.[5] Encouraged by his success in Iran, Eisenhower used the CIA to overturn a government in Guatemala. Guatemalan president Jacobo Arbenz Guzman had instituted an agrarian reform law that seized unused land to distribute to peasants. When his government appropriated four hundred thousand acres owned by the United Fruit Company, a U.S. firm, Eisenhower proved receptive to company lobbyists and State Department warnings of communist influence. After Arbenz sought Soviet military aid, Eisenhower authorized a covert CIA operation.

The CIA combined an army of mercenaries from the United States and Central America with Guatemalan soldiers who were trained in Florida. In June 1954, this mixed band of less than two thousand warriors left a base in Honduras and entered Guatemala. Arbenz countered by threatening to arm the peasants, but his tactic backfired. More threatened by the prospect of an armed peasant militia than by the invading force, his army chiefs demanded his resignation, and Arbenz fled the country. It was an easy victory for the CIA, which encouraged them to "Guatemalize" other recalcitrant neighbors in the future.

Guatemala and Iran were peripheral during Eisenhower's first term. Relations with the Soviet Union remained central. With the death of Soviet leader Josef Stalin in 1953, a thaw in the Cold War seemed possible. At first there was an encouraging signal from Stalin's successor, Georgy Malenkov, who suggested, in April 1953, that both sides meet to negotiate mutual troop reductions in Europe. His overture was rebuffed with a threat of further Western rearmament if the Soviets failed to cooperate in ending revolts in Asia, reunifying Germany, allowing political change in Eastern Europe, and facilitating Austrian independence. In short, the Cold War just turned more frigid under Eisenhower.[6]

With no chance of an early relaxation of tensions between the superpowers and their allies, both sides accelerated their pace of weapon development. The United States exploded a thermonuclear hydrogen bomb in March 1954, and the Soviets detonated their H-bomb the following fall. Now both sides recognized the danger of nuclear holocaust and agreed to a summit conference. In July 1955, the new Soviet prime minister, Nikolay Bulganin, met with Eisenhower in Geneva. There Eisenhower presented his "open skies" proposal, which provided for mutual aerial inspection of nuclear facilities. Nikita Khrushchev, the Soviet party secretary, who accompanied Bulganin, rejected the plan as nothing more than a device to spy on the Soviet Union. The Geneva Conference ended with no agreement on disarmament or on any other major issue. Thus the Cold War and the arms race continued in Eisenhower's first term in office.

Later, during his second term, tension with the Soviet Union increased when nationalism in Eastern Europe and the Middle East exploded. In June 1956, an uprising in Poland ended only when Wladyslaw Gomulka assumed power and reformed the secret police. When the Soviets protested, Gomulka threatened to encourage a popular uprising. Khrushchev, now prime minister of the Soviet Union, relented, which encouraged anticommunist riots in Hungary. This time Soviet tanks suppressed the incipient revolution. Eisenhower's Secretary of State, John Foster Dulles, had advocated the liberation of Eastern Europe. But the president did nothing to help the Hungarians.

Eisenhower confronted an almost simultaneous crisis in the Middle East. As Soviet tanks entered Hungary, British, French, and Israeli forces moved against Egypt in 1956. The crisis was rooted in the Egyptian nationalism that had emerged in 1952, when Colonel Gamal Abdel Nasser led an army coup against King Farouk. Nasser wanted to strengthen his army and the Egyptian economy. With American financial support, he planned an Aswan dam to use the water of the lower Nile to provide electric power and open new farmland. At first the United States agreed to help, but when Dulles learned that Nasser was buying Czechoslovak weapons and had formed a military alliance with Saudi Arabia, Syria, and Yemen, he withdrew U.S. funding for the dam. Nasser responded by nationalizing the Suez Canal.

For a time, Nasser kept the canal open, but by October British and French dissatisfaction grew and they conspired with Israel to invade Egypt. On October 29, 1956, Israel attacked and the French and British entered the fight, ostensibly to protect the canal, which by that time had been closed by sunken ships. Within three days, British and French forces occupied the territory bordering the canal and ordered Israeli and Egyptian troops to withdraw.

The tripartite invaders fooled no one. There was an outcry from other powers, including the United States and the Soviet Union. The United Nations expressed universal condemnation when it passed a resolution demanding a cease-fire. The United States exerted additional pressure on Britain and France by appealing to Latin American oil producers to deny petroleum to the invaders. The combination of censure and boycott worked. British and French forces withdrew, and Israel surrendered the territory it held in Sinai and Gaza when the United Nations pledged to create an armed buffer zone between the two countries and protect Israel's access to the Red Sea.

Eisenhower reacted to the Suez crisis by asking Congress, in January 1957, to authorize him to use force to stop communist penetration in the Middle East. Like the Truman Doctrine, Eisenhower's doctrine capitalized on the fear of communism to increase his war-making powers. A year later he invoked the doctrine when the president of Lebanon appealed to the United States to help suppress a civil war. Eisenhower obliged and sent fourteen thousand troops. This show of force had the immediate effect of preventing Iraq from joining Nasser's United Arab Republic alliance and of discouraging overt Soviet support of Egypt.[7] In the longer term, Eisenhower, like Truman, set another precedent for using force without a declaration of war.

Using American troops in Lebanon deviated from Eisenhower's New Look defense policy, which de-emphasized the use of conventional military action. The administration wanted to get "more bang for the buck" by relying on nuclear weapons and thereby saving American lives and money. Additionally, when the Soviets launched the first space satellite, *Sputnik*, on October 4, 1957, it was feared they could also hurl intercontinental ballistic missiles against the United States. Talk of missile gap and missile crisis was pervasive, and as the shopping list for strategic weapons grew, allocations for conventional warfare were further reduced. As a result, the Army and the Marine Corps had to economize.

For conventional warriors, the last years of the Eisenhower administration were grim financially, and for the Marines there were the added burdens of public scandal and private strife. Of paramount importance was finding an appropriate successor to Commandant Randolph McC. Pate. The Corps needed an officer who could polish its tarnished image, end internal and external politicking, and maintain combat readiness with less money and fewer troops. That unenviable task fell to a most unlikely candidate for the position, General David M. Shoup.[8]

Shoup understood the political reasons for his selection. It was clear that Secretary of Defense Thomas S. Gates wanted him to clean house, to rid the Corps of the politicos. Possibly, as General Megee recalls, Shoup's selection was a compromise appointment to avoid choosing among the frontrunners.[9] It is more likely that Gates wanted an independent leader who "was free of any alliances or any cluttering up of people. He didn't bring any boys along with him . . . he was a free agent and a man with a tremendous record and we thought that image would be the kind of image the Marine Corps ought to return to."[10] General Lewis W. Walt made a number of astute observations on the matter. Before the announcement of Shoup's appointment, he predicted, "I believe General T. will lose because of Navy opposition to him. I don't believe he has Mr. Gates's support . . . Mr. Gates, I believe appreciates the political situation in the M.C. and doesn't want another 'team' member as C.M.C. You have been built up as a non-team combat Marine."[11]

Shoup denied that he intended to "adopt the massive new broomation policy" in his first "Remarks by Commandant of the Marine Corps to Staff on January 4, 1960."[12] He also used the occasion to take a shot at the Chowder Society and others who felt the Corps was being victimized. Shoup admonished Marines to "unshackle our minds from the stifling psychology inherent in the slogan 'They're sniping at us,' [and] . . . let us rid ourselves of any fear of occupying any inferior status in the national defense establishment."[13]

These first "Remarks" hit their target. Twining retired immediately, and all the other lieutenant generals who had been senior to Shoup resigned as well. Sometimes Shoup encouraged officers to leave by signaling to them they would not receive an important assignment. One prominent exception was General Krulak, who remained to command the Recruit Depot in San Diego. Krulak was pleased to be some distance from Headquarters because he was disappointed that Twining had not been selected to be commandant. And Shoup knew it. For that reason and others there was always a certain tension between Shoup and Krulak. But Krulak's career did not suffer. He continued to serve in a variety of important posts.

Shoup was determined to end internal politicking as well. Before Shoup became commandant, it was commonplace for junior officers to join "teams," to attach themselves to a senior officer who could shield them from career-killing mistakes and assign them to career-building work. Shoup ended that practice. He also reined in the Chowder Society, disparaged by some Marines as the First Division Gang because they appeared to enjoy a privileged position in the Corps. Justified or not, Shoup made sure that everyone understood that no individual or group would receive preferential treatment. Assignments would be based on need and merit.

Shoup was not a gentle reformer. His style was abrasive and often cruel. He was particularly hard on senior officers, whom he sometimes "chewed out" in the presence of subordinates, a serious breach of military decorum. An officer once told Mrs. Shoup, "You never have to worry about your husband getting ulcers. He just causes them in others."[14] It may have been Shoup's method of getting information that caused those ulcers. He favored interrogating officers, and if they did not have their facts straight, he excoriated them with profanity.

Even friends suffered. On one occasion, he chastised General Weiseman for not having sufficient information. Weiseman held his ground and told Shoup bluntly that he had no intention of memorizing every detail in every report. Shoup backed down, but the incident reveals that he was not always an officer and a gentleman.

Shoup was a tough, no-nonsense marine whose earthy, sometimes crude, behavior was always evident. He liked to remind people of his humble background, and whenever he thought someone was trying to deceive him or acting foolishly, he would proclaim, "Well, I wouldn't know. I'm just an Indiana plowboy." Then he would unload a barrage of verbal abuse. He was uncommonly common and detested the superior attitude of some marines. Soon after he became commandant, he made the swagger stick an "optional piece of attire" because he thought carrying one was an elitist affectation.[15] It also reminded him of the arrogant British officers he had seen in China who struck coolies with their swagger sticks. Everyone understood their options, and the sticks disappeared.

Officers who worked closely with Shoup tolerated his harsh treatment because they knew he loved the Corps and they understood the challenges confronting him. He had to rebuild the Marine Corps with scant resources. When Shoup was named commandant, the Marine Corps's budget decreased from $942 million in 1959 to $902 million in 1961. The allocation for 1961 provided funds for only a 175,000-man Corps, when 200,000 troops were needed.[16]

New Look economizing did not trouble Shoup. He believed that "Ike was forced to make cuts because the original estimates that came in from the armed forces . . . [were] so ridiculous. I would say ludicrous. But most of that is because they had no directive. They had no national security policy to play their game against."[17] Shoup was convinced the remedy was to "tell them . . . in a national security policy directive to the Defense Department, that your forces be limited to the capabilities as follows, and set forth what they should be capable of doing. And then you can build a budget on that. That's a policy. We've never had it. . . . I feel so sincere about this, I think I'm right, and that this engendered the snowballing of the military-industrial complex."[18] Like Eisenhower, Shoup believed that defense spending was controlled by a dangerous alliance.

Shoup believed the misalliance included the armaments industry and Congress. Weapons manufacturers were culpable because they retained large research staffs, which developed superfluous technology to preserve their jobs. The result, in Shoup's opinion, was "the next thing you know you've bought a God damned piece of hardware that . . . wouldn't be but a very small percentage better than what you had." He believed Congress was at fault too because it "was so tied up politically. In other words, you get a gunpowder factory and . . . the thing for that politician to do is to do everything in his power to get that factory in his state. That means votes. That's all it is."[19]

Shoup shared Eisenhower's anxiety over the growing military-industrial complex that bloated defense spending. But he did not agree with other aspects of the New Look, particularly the administration's policy in Southeast Asia. Shoup viewed the domino theory as an "over-exaggeration," based on the assumption "that all the peoples must surely and properly think of things the way we do." The Southeast Asian people did not want American aid to resist communism.

Shoup believed too that foreign aid really did not work anywhere in the world. Even in its most benign and benevolent forms, it was unwanted. When Shoup was in Morocco, he observed how American aid was used to construct beautiful little stucco houses with tile roofs for people accustomed to living in mud huts. The Moroccans never moved in. They put their livestock in the new buildings and continued to live in their mud huts "happy as hell."[20]

On other important defense matters, Shoup agreed with the administration. He admired, for example, the way Eisenhower handled the so-called missile-gap complaint that emerged as an important issue in the 1960 presidential campaign. For more than two years, Eisenhower tried to reassure the American people that "long-range ballistic missiles as they exist today do not cancel the destructive power of our Strategic Air Force."[21] But it was to no avail. Prominent journalists, like Joe Alsop, and powerful senators, like Stuart Symington of Missouri, had already sounded the alarm. John F. Kennedy merely capitalized on the widespread anxiety over missile strength.

Shoup was unperturbed, and he liked the way Eisenhower handled the missile misery that affected the country. He thought Eisenhower was prophetic. "He could see the blooming," Shoup recalled. "Pretty soon we get to where we have enough warheads to blow both nations off the map ten or twelve times. It's that kind of thing—the overkill ability. Even giving each nation, with its anti-missiles and anti-missile missiles and all that, give them some credit for a certain amount of kills, we still can do it. They can devastate this nation and we can devastate there, no doubt about it. And if we wait long enough China can do it to both of us."[22] Shoup shared Eisenhower's concern that there were other more important things to worry about.

What worried both Shoup and Eisenhower was the growing power of the military-industrial complex. In his farewell address to the American people on January 17, 1959, Eisenhower warned: "In the councils of government we must guard against the acquisition of unwarranted influence, whether sought or unsought, by the military-industrial complex. The potential for the disastrous rise of misplaced power exists and will persist."[23] The comment reflected a widespread belief that militarism was overtaking the country. Three years earlier a prominent and popular sociologist, C. Wright Mills, in his book *The Power Elite*, described American militarism as "the attempt of military men to increase their powers, and hence their status, in comparison with businessmen and politicians. To gain such powers they must not be considered a mere means to be used by politicians and moneymakers. . . . On the contrary, their ends must be identified with the ends as well as the honor of the nation."[24]

Taken to the extreme, a popular general might take over the country. That idea was the theme of a popular novel published shortly after Eisenhower left office. Two journalists, Fletcher Knebel and Charles W. Bailey II, in their novel *Seven Days in May*, describe a conspiracy by a popular general and a powerful senator to take over the United States. Shoup saw himself depicted in that story. When he was asked about civilian control over the military Shoup replied, "Without that, we're sunk." Referring to the book he commented: "*Eight* [sic] *Days in May* or whatever it is, in which one of the fellows in there was supposed to be Shoup [the authors portray that] our system would never permit, encourage, or develop anything in which the armed forces would become a competitor with the U.S. government for control of America. Oh no. We've never had that and I'm quite certain we never will have it."[25] In any event Shoup felt that "Ike never intended to let the armed forces get control of America."

Nevertheless, intended or not, the policies of the Eisenhower administration, with its penchant for confrontation, took the country to the precipice of world war. In his book, *The Causes of World War Three*, C. Wright Mills referred to the "crackpot realism" in the Eisenhower administration where "high-flying moral rhetoric" was leading the country to conflagration.[26] It remained to be seen if saner realists, like Shoup, would prevail and influence the incoming administration.

Notes

1. C. Wright Mills, *The Causes of World War Three* (New York, 1960), 89.
2. See John Lewis Gaddis, *Strategies of Containment: A Critical Appraisal of Postwar American National Security Policy* (New York, 1982), chapter 5. Dwight

D. Eisenhower, *The White House Years: Waging Peace, 1959–1961* (Garden City, N.Y., 1965), 16. The background material for this chapter is based on the excellent account in Allan R. Millett and Peter Maslowski, *For the Common Defense: A Military History of the United States of America* (New York: Free Press, 1984).

3. See Geoffrey Perret, *Eisenhower* (New York, 1999), chapter 35.

4. Richard H. Immerman, *John Foster Dulles: Piety, Pragmatism, and Power in U.S. Foreign Policy* (Wilmington, Del., 1999), 121–24.

5. Perret, *Eisenhower*, 478–79.

6. See Richard Immerman, *The CIA in Guatemala: The Foreign Policy of Intervention* (Austin, 1982).

7. Gaddis, *Strategies of Containment*, 177–78.

8. Millett, *Semper Fidelis*, 544.

9. Vernon E. Megee, Oral History Transcript, HQMC History Division, 1973, 229.

10. Thomas S. Gates interview with the author, May 26, 1982.

11. Lewis W. Walt to David M. Shoup, June 27, 1959, Shoup Papers.

12. Shoup file, Marine Corps Historical Center, 1. Lt. Gen. Robert E. Hogaboom believed that he was encouraged to leave. See Hogaboom Oral History Transcript, HQMC, History Division, 1972, 342, 343, 346. All five lieutenant generals retired: Vernon E. Megee, Edwin A. Pollock, Merrill B. Twining, Robert E. Hogaboom (all effective November 1, 1959), and Verne J. McCaul (effective January 1, 1960); Major General Roy M. Gulick and Brigadier General William W. Stickney retired effective January 1, 1960. Shoup consulted with others before making his selections for the important billets. See Victor H. Krulak to David M. Shoup, August 20, 1959; Frederick L. Weiseman to David M. Shoup, August 20, 1959; T. A. Wornham to David M. Shoup, August 22, 1959; Robert Hogaboom to David M. Shoup, August 24, 1959, all in Shoup Papers.

13. Shoup file, Marine Corps Historical Center, 1.

14. Mrs. Zola Shoup, interview with the author, February 28, 1980, Alexandria, Virginia.

15. General Edwin H. Simmons, interview with the author, February 27, 1990.

16. Millett, *Semper Fidelis*, 533.

17. Millett, *Semper Fidelis*, 533.

18. David M. Shoup, Transcript, "Eisenhower Administration," Columbia University Oral History Research Office, 1973, 25.

19. Shoup, Transcript, 21.

20. Shoup, Transcript, 28.

21. Perret, *Eisenhower*, 560.

22. Shoup, Transcript, 21.

23. Eisenhower, *White House Years*, 614.

24. C. Wright Mills, *The Power Elite* (New York, 1956).

25. Shoup, Transcript, 23–24.

26. Mills, *Causes of World War Three*, 89.

6

Rational Realism

Foreign policy was central to the presidential campaign of 1960, though the contest was more a question of style than substance. Both John F. Kennedy and Richard M. Nixon accepted the underlying assumptions of containment thinking that had dominated the Truman and Eisenhower administrations.[1] Kennedy attacked Eisenhower and Nixon for losing the Cold War: for allowing a strategic deficit (the "missile gap") for losing the Third World to communism, for embarrassment in confrontations with the Soviets, and for allowing an imbalance in trade. Kennedy's narrow victory, however, was not a triumph of issues but a tribute to his energy, good looks, charm, and captivating speeches.

Once elected, Kennedy set out to prove that his administration was smarter and tougher than his predecessor's. He surrounded himself with advisers who were intellectual activists. Not since the Franklin D. Roosevelt years had a president included so many academics in positions of power. His inner circle included McGeorge Bundy, historian and former Harvard dean, as the national security adviser. Bundy was to play a major role in centralizing foreign policy in the White House. For Secretary of Defense he chose Robert S. McNamara, a statistically minded former executive from Ford Motor Company. McNamara's mastery of statistical decision making transformed the Department of Defense and helped make him a towering figure in national security deliberations. Finally, the Attorney General, Robert F. Kennedy, the president's brother, friend, and confidant, undertook special assignments.[2]

Kennedy wanted to be his own Secretary of State, and for that reason he avoided the more prestigious aspirants for the job and selected Dean Rusk, head of the Rockefeller Foundation. Rusk was intelligent and had State Department experience, but he lacked the assertiveness and vigor of Kennedy's policy entourage. For the most part, Rusk was ignored.

Kennedy's approach to policy making was vastly different from Eisenhower's. Unlike Eisenhower, he bypassed the National Security Council and relied instead on the advice of trusted advisers with whom he met intermittently to solve specific problems. The informal approach had the effect of diminishing the role of the Joint Chiefs of Staff in security matters. For Shoup, whose role in the Joint Chiefs of Staff was limited to begin with, it promised even less influence.

The Joint Chiefs of Staff position in policy making deteriorated further as a result of the Bay of Pigs fiasco. Kennedy blamed them for not warning him sufficiently of the dangers of a secret invasion of Cuba. In this instance, as in others, Kennedy failed to carefully reexamine an Eisenhower initiative. The plan to remove Castro first appeared in October 1959, when Eisenhower approved a scheme conceived by the State Department and the CIA to encourage anti-Castro groups in Cuba. It envisioned assisting Cuban exiles in attacking Cuba from U.S. territory.[3] Later, in January 1960, the CIA created a Task Force WH/4, Branch 4 of the Western Hemisphere Division, to carry out the plan under the direction of Jacob Esterline, former Guatemalan station chief, who had engineered the operation to overthrow the Arbenz government. By March 1960, plans had sufficiently crystallized for Eisenhower to make the plan official. On March 17, he approved the CIA paper "A Program of Covert Action against the Castro Regime." The paper reported that a secret operation was under way to develop a paramilitary force outside Cuba to conduct a covert military operation on the island. An integral part of the plan was a modest but expandable air capability for resupply and infiltration to be organized secretly in another country.[4] The policy document did not mention involving the Joint Chiefs or any of the services. It was entirely a CIA operation.

During the presidential campaign in the summer of 1960, CIA director Allen Dulles visited Kennedy at the family summer compound in Hyannis Port and disclosed that Cuban exiles were being trained to attack Castro.[5] The revelation did not stop Kennedy from attacking the Eisenhower administration in October for allowing a communist state to emerge just ninety miles from the United States. And he advocated strengthening "anti-Castro forces in exile and in Cuba itself who offer eventual hope of overthrowing Castro."[6]

At that juncture, in October, Commandant Shoup told Colonel Jack Hawkins that the CIA planned to land exiles in Cuba and had asked that a Marine colonel be assigned to the operation. Shoup complied and sent Hawkins "there on a temporary basis."[7] Hawkins was designated the paramilitary expert, and joined Esterline in planning the covert operation.

In the following month, November, the CIA altered its plan, changing the operation from one of guerrilla infiltration to an amphibious invasion requiring at least fifteen hundred men with conventional military training.[8] At the same time, CIA director Allen Dulles and his deputy director of plans, Richard Bissell, visited Kennedy and briefed him on the scheme to overthrow Castro.

After Kennedy was elected, Eisenhower met with him in January to encourage the president-elect to continue the operation against Castro. Kennedy also met with the Joint Chiefs that month and learned from General Lyman Lemnitzer that Cuba had received more than thirty thousand tons of arms from Czechoslovakia, which meant that the planned covert force would not be strong enough. On January 27, 1961, the Joint Chiefs sent a memorandum to Kennedy asserting that Cuba appeared to be part of the communist bloc and Castro should be eliminated, but they doubted that the current paramilitary plan was the solution. Alternatively, they recommended that an Inter Departmental Planning Group be established to design a more appropriate response.

A better approach was outlined in a report by the Joint Chiefs, "JCSM 57-61, Military Evaluation of the CIA Paramilitary Plan for Cuba." This report concluded that an invading force might succeed initially but could not prevail without a popular uprising or additional forces. Even so, the report cautioned that this judgment was not based on firsthand observation of the combat ability of the invaders and that further evaluations should be made by representatives from the Army, Navy and Air Force. Still, the Joint Chiefs did provide a lukewarm endorsement of the plan, giving it merely a "fair" chance of success.[9]

Essentially, the plan they endorsed was the work of Jacob Esterline and Jack Hawkins, who felt that success depended upon two conditions. Esterline believed that everything hinged on the assumption that a large uprising would follow the invasion. Hawkins added that control of the air must be achieved before the force was landed; otherwise the whole enterprise was doomed.[10] Their design, the Trinidad Plan, was vetoed by the State Department.

On several occasions, Colonel Hawkins accompanied Dulles to the White House to meet with Kennedy and members of his cabinet to discuss the operation. From the outset, Secretary of State Rusk objected to the plan, particularly the use of aircraft. Hawkins was appalled and thought that someone needed to explain to Rusk that an amphibious landing was impossible without air cover. In any event, Kennedy rejected the plan as being too noisy and looking like an invasion. Kennedy and the State Department insisted upon seizing an airfield capable of supporting B-26 bombers on the first day to provide a base for air support. The CIA was given just three days to revise their plan with the new stipulation.

Despite the short notice, the CIA drew up plans for three alternative invasion sites and presented them to the Joint Chiefs of Staff on March 14 and 15. Of the three options, the Joint Chiefs supported the one involving an invasion at Zapata Peninsula on the Bay of Pigs. They noted that all three alternatives, including the Bay of Pigs, were inferior to the Trinidad Plan and less likely to succeed. CIA planners Esterline and Hawkins agreed. They also preferred the more isolated Trinidad location because the landing beaches were accessible and mountains to the west and a river to the north and east would protect the invaders. The two bridges spanning the river could be easily destroyed, thereby preventing Castro's tanks and vehicles from counterattacking. If all else failed, the attackers could flee to the mountains.

Hawkins warned Bissell that an attacking force at the Bay of Pigs could hold the beaches for only a short time and that, if they were overwhelmed, there was no place for them to run. In Hawkins's estimation, the Bay of Pigs target was a mistake and "Mr. Bissell acted unwisely in not defending the Trinidad operation. If they wanted to get rid of Castro, he should have defended that, 'cause that was the only chance."[11] Hawkins also denounced Bissell's failure to "defend the need for air operations . . . the president had never really been informed about the necessity for eliminating Castro's air forces."[12] Hawkins and Esterline were so disgusted with the course of events that they went to Bissell's house in April to resign because they were convinced the Bay of Pigs invasion would fail. Bissell persuaded them to remain with an assurance that he would ask Kennedy to authorize sufficient air strength.

Esterline and Hawkins were not the only critics of the Bay of Pigs operation in March and April. On March 30, the chairman of the Senate Foreign Relations Committee, William Fulbright, went to Florida to hand Kennedy in person a long memorandum warning that the American role could not be concealed and "would have undone the work of thirty years in trying to live down earlier interventions."[13] Likewise, Under Secretary of State Chester Bowles submitted a memorandum to Rusk stating, "the chances of success are not greater than one out of three. This makes it a highly risky operation."[14] One of Kennedy's closest advisers, Arthur Schlesinger Jr., sent a memorandum on April 4 terming the invasion "a terrible idea."[15]

Surprisingly, in the final days before the scheduled landing, Hawkins was optimistic. In reply to an inquiry from Esterline about the effectiveness of the paramilitary force, Hawkins wrote: "they have supreme confidence they will win all engagements against the best Castro has to offer." Apparently Bissell showed Hawkins's evaluation to Kennedy, which persuaded the president to continue with the planned invasion. But during a meeting with Bissell on April 14, Kennedy cut in half the number of planes to be used in the air strike. Bissell later recalled that he did not think Kennedy understood how critical the air strikes were to the success of the invasion.[16]

While the first phase of the operation was already under way on April 16, National Security Adviser McGeorge Bundy telephoned General Cabell of the CIA and told him that the second air strike scheduled for dawn on D-Day could not be launched until the planes could take off from the captured airstrip at the Bay of Pigs. The change in plans incensed Cabell, and he immediately went with Bissell to see Rusk to protest the decision. In their presence, Rusk called Kennedy, noting their objections and restating his position that the morning strike should be cancelled. He offered to let them speak to Kennedy, but they refused. Later in the day, Cabell called Kennedy again to lobby for the air strikes but was turned down.[17]

The air attack began on April 15 against aircraft at Campo Libertad, San Antonio, and Santiago. Reports varied, but by one conservative estimate, half of Castro's tactical air force of fifteen to eighteen aircraft was destroyed—not enough to prevent a serious threat to the landing force. The next day when Hawkins learned from Esterline that the president, following the advice of the State Department, had cancelled further air strikes, he contacted the CIA. He urged Bissell "in the strongest terms that the President be immediately requested to reconsider this decision and that the possible disastrous consequences of canceling these attacks be explained to him."[18] Hawkins predicted that supply ships would be sunk, because Castro retained sufficient aircraft to inflict terrible damage. Had he known earlier that the air attacks had been cancelled, Hawkins would have urged that the operation be stopped. By the time he learned of the president's decision, it was too late. The ships were already approaching the rendezvous area off the beaches. Only one option remained and that was to resume the air strikes.

Hawkins was frantic and appealed to Shoup. Shoup remembered,

> I was called on the telephone about, it must have been 1:30 in the
> morning, the night of the fiasco. And this colonel [Hawkins] I re-
> ferred to was crying and said, "General, you've got to get a hold of
> the President because they have influenced him to call off the air
> strike." He was crying, but of course I said, "Well, has he already
> made his decision?" He said, "Yes, they told us we're not going to
> do it." I said, "Well, Christ knows that I can't do anything. Maybe if
> I'd had a chance beforehand." Well, he was very evasive and made
> some comment about the U.N. chief and the Secretary of State. It
> was all so mixed up that I never got it straightened out from him.
> And I don't know whether I have it straightened out. All I know is
> that the President of the United States said, "Okay, don't use the air
> power." And I have closed the chapter on the Bay of Pigs—and I
> think quite properly so, except maybe for a few things. When the
> President of the United States publicly to America said, "I'm at
> fault," I think that ought to end it.[19]

Even if Shoup had succeeded in getting through to the president,
it is unlikely that his appeal would have changed Kennedy's mind.
Others had tried and failed.

The failure to employ adequate air cover doomed the mission.
The obsolete B-26 bombers used by the invaders were no match for
Castro's remaining jet aircraft, which quickly destroyed the supply
freighters, *Rio Escondido* and *Houston*, and frightened off other ships
destined for the landing area. Left without supplies, the attacking
brigade soon succumbed to Castro's combined force of tanks, artillery, and aircraft. By 2:00 p.m. on April 19, the exile brigade had surrendered.

After the defeat, on April 21, Kennedy accepted responsibility for
the failure of the invasion, but that did not end the matter. The following day he appointed an investigation team headed by General
Maxwell D. Taylor, Attorney General Robert Kennedy, and CIA Director Allen Dulles. Hearings started within weeks, and Shoup was
among the witnesses called to testify. On May 8, Shoup testified before
the committee. He prefaced his remarks with a summary of his feelings about the entire operation. To begin with, he reported that he
"went through the NSC [National Security Council] papers and discovered that the national policy was the overthrow of the Castro
regime."[20] With that in mind, the CIA drew up the Trinidad Plan and
asked the Joint Chiefs to evaluate it. After carefully looking at the mission of the operation, which was to land and distribute arms to people
who would lead an uprising to overthrow Castro, Shoup concurred
with the opinion of other members of the Joint Chiefs that the plan

would work. Later, when the Trinidad Plan was abandoned because the president thought it looked like a World War II invasion, the CIA developed alternatives. The additional presidential stipulation that an airfield be captured left only one viable choice, the Zapata region. Of the alternatives being considered, there was no doubt in anyone's mind that the Zapata had the greatest chance of success. "However," Shoup added, "one thought was predominant. You must achieve air superiority or you are not going to be able to get ashore."[21]

When he was asked about the chances of success of the operation, he replied that if the plan had been carried out, it should have accomplished the mission. He went on to say, "I very frankly made this statement, if this kind of an operation can be done with the kind of force with this much training and knowledge about it, then we are wasting our time in our divisions, we ought to go on leave for three months out of four."[22] Queried if his statement contradicted his favorable assessment of the prospects of the operation, he replied that it did not.[23]

Shoup was questioned repeatedly about the military responsibility for the failure of the operation. He replied by denying that anyone on the Joint Chiefs was responsible. As advisers to the president, he admitted that the Joint Chiefs had an obligation to advise the president within the limits of their knowledge of the plan. And he added, disingenuously, "I want to tell you this right now. Had I as an individual heard that they were going to call off the air strikes, I'd have asked that the Commander in Chief be informed. I'd have called him myself because it [the air strikes] was absolutely essential to success."[24] Shoup never revealed he had neglected to respond to Colonel Hawkins's plea that he ask the president to reinstate the air strikes on the morning of D-Day.

At the end of his testimony, Shoup spoke candidly about the covert nature of the operation. He was asked, "If you were going to do this again and there was still the requirement that it be a covert operation, what changes would you make?" Shoup answered, "I don't think that at this time in 1961 or hereafter you are going to do it covertly."[25] His observation was later incorporated into the Taylor committee's report.

On June 13, the report was presented to the president. The document identified the lack of ammunition as the immediate cause of failure. The ammunition shortage was the result of poor fire discipline, the loss of two supply ships, *Rio Escondido* and *Houston*, and the hasty retreat of other supporting vessels. But the most serious failure of the operation according to the committee was the decision to cancel the air strikes at dawn on D-Day. They suggested that "the cancellation seems to have resulted partly from the failure to make the air strike plan entirely clear in advance to the President and the Secretary of State, but, more importantly, by misgivings as to the effect of the air strikes on the position of the United States in the current UN debate on Cuba. Finally, there was the failure to carry the issue to the President when the opportunity was presented and explain to him with proper force the probable military consequences of a last minute cancellation."[26]

Clearly, the last failure was attributed to the Joint Chiefs, and there were specific recommendations to remedy this weakness. The report suggested that the president notify the Joint Chiefs of Staff that "he expects their advice to come to him direct and unfiltered."[27] And in a swipe at the chairman, General Lemnitzer, the report went on to say that "when only the Chairman or a single Chief is present, that officer must represent the Chiefs as a body . . . to assure that he does in fact represent the corporate judgment of the Joint Chiefs of Staff." This recommendation may have been prompted by Shoup's testimony, whose understanding of the mission of the operation differed from that of other chiefs. When Shoup was asked how long he thought the invaders would be in the Bay of Pigs, he said one day.[28] Later, during the questioning, a member of the committee stated, "It's very significant that the Commandant of the Marine Corps, whom the President of the United States and the Secretary of State thought had approved this plan, had an entirely different idea of what the plan was. It seems that something has gone wrong somewhere along the line."[29] Apparently he, the interrogator, was referring to the testimony of another member of the Joint Chiefs, admiral Arleigh A. Burke, who stated that "the only slight difference I have with General Shoup is that it was my understanding that this group had to be able to hold a beachhead for some time, for several days."[30] The committee did not see that difference as slight and made note of it in their recommendations.

Shoup's reaction to the criticism of the Joint Chiefs was that it was "unjustly and unfairly [made] because, in the first place, it was shoved in their laps. . . . We weren't given this on the basis of what do you recommend. . . . We were given this on the basis of, 'You help us do it. You help get this thing on the road and get it done.'"[31] Shoup did not believe the Joint Chiefs were responsible. "I don't think," he recalled, "any of the Joint Chiefs could have rightfully taken a position to argue with a Presidential decision. They weren't asked to tell us why we ought to stop this now. I don't ever remember being approached on that basis."[32] If anyone were to blame, Shoup argued, it was the CIA. "As far as I'm concerned, this jars my first experience of knowing what kind of machination that the CIA could get into. I'll be absolutely honest about it; I didn't know they went in for this kind of thing. Soon I was astounded, first, that they would be in this kind of business to that extent . . . to develop an invasion force without the know-how and all the experience and backing of a military force. And so, as far as the success of it was concerned . . . I just didn't believe it could be successful. I knew it couldn't be successful if they kept on dallying about the air."[33]

Shoup did not believe that the Bay of Pigs led to a crisis of confidence in the Joint Chiefs. "I never felt that way," he recalled, "and I never heard it expressed."[34] He also rejected the notion that Maxwell Taylor was appointed the military adviser to the president because Kennedy was dissatisfied with the Joint Chiefs, but the president's subsequent behavior proved him wrong. Kennedy always paid the Joint Chiefs the courtesy of asking for their opinion, but he took private council with Taylor and other trusted advisers. In time, Shoup would play a similar role. In the aftermath of the Bay of Pigs crisis, the administration held the Joint Chiefs in low esteem.

To overcome the crisis in confidence that emerged between the president and the Joint Chiefs, Kennedy created a new White House position, military representative of the president. What he had in mind was an officer to be "my advisor to see that I am not making a dumb mistake as Commander in Chief."[35] He selected the now retired General Taylor and assigned him first to investigate the Bay of Pigs debacle. Kennedy had invited Taylor to Washington on April 21 to offer him the new post as his military adviser. He was careful in describing the duties of the new position to add sufficient qualifications to prevent Congress and others from accusing him of trying to circumvent the statutory duties of the Joint Chiefs. But it was clear that the military representative would provide advice and act as a liaison officer with the Defense Department, intelligence agencies, and the Joint Chiefs. In his capacity as an officer "available to represent the President when the latter desires senior military representation at home or abroad," the advisor's potential power was great.

Taylor's appointment also signaled a radical departure from the previous administration's defense policy. Kennedy had first become acquainted with Taylor when he read his book *The Uncertain Trumpet*.[36] The book was a bitter denunciation of Eisenhower's New Look defense policy. In place of massive retaliation and its reliance on strategic deterrence, Taylor advanced his alternative strategy, flexible response. Taylor wrote:

> The strategic doctrine which I would propose to replace Massive Re-
> taliation is called herein the Strategy of Flexible Response. This
> name suggests the need for a capability to react across the entire
> spectrum of possible challenge, for coping with anything from gen-
> eral atomic war to infiltrations and aggressions as threatened Laos
> and Berlin in 1959. The new strategy would recognize that it is just
> as necessary to deter or win quickly a limited war as to deter general
> war. Otherwise, the limited war which we cannot win quickly may
> result in our piecemeal attrition or involvement in an expanding
> conflict which may grow into the general war we all want to avoid.[37]

His flexible-response strategy became the basis of Kennedy's national defense policy.

Kennedy's flexible-response policy emphasized expanding conventional forces. That approach led to an increase in Marine Corps troop strength from 175,000 to 190,000 and a $67 million-budget increase. Additional funds were also made available to the Corps as a result of secretary of Defense Robert S. McNamara's system of allocating funds by military function, not branch of service. That meant the Corps now drew its funds from the General Purpose Forces fund instead of receiving a portion of the allotment to the Navy.

Unfortunately, the new system proved to be an embarrassment of riches because it revealed weaknesses in the Corps' accounting methods. There was no centralized inventory control. Marine Corps Headquarters in Washington, D.C., and the Philadelphia supply depot divided procurement and storage accounting responsibilities; Headquarters recorded expenditures on expensive items; the supply depot recorded expenditures on replacement parts and the more voluminous war materials. This division of responsibility was so chaotic that the Fleet Marine Force never knew what it had or what it needed.

Shoup solved the supply problem in two ways. First, he implemented data processing in administration. Under his direction, the Corps developed an inventory management system that applied modern data-processing techniques to supply, disbursement, and depot management.

The second, and arguably more profound, innovation was the elimination of the Supply-Duty Only (SDO) category of personnel, which promoted efficiency and racial equality. Shoup was aware that morale was low in the Supply Service because SDO officers were second-class marines. They were restricted in their assignments and were ineligible for promotion to the highest ranks. Many supply officers were African American, which prompted many marines to refer to SDOs as the Black Brotherhood.[38] That casual observation was documented in a disparaging 1963 report of a presidential committee on equal opportunity in the Armed Forces. The report observed, "Many of the Negroes in the Navy and the Marine Corps are still grouped in assignments which perpetuate the image of the Negro as a menial or servant in respect to the total activities of these Services, and it will take some time before the more recent assignment trends rectify this discrepancy."[39] Consequently, when Shoup ended the caste-like treatment of supply personnel, he simultaneously promoted racial equality in the Corps. His efforts culminated in legislation that created a new branch of the Corps that embraced supply, financial management, and logistical support. Officers who served in the new branch were not limited in promotion or restricted in assignments. In this way, Shoup promoted justice and efficiency in the Corps.[40]

The new administration's approach to national security afforded the Marine Corps a singular opportunity to improve its relations with the president, Congress, and the other services. In time, Shoup would become one of Kennedy's favorite generals, second only to Maxwell Taylor. When one of Shoup's generals at Headquarters was asked how the Corps stood with the new administration, Lieutenant General Charles H. Hayes recalled, "I think quite well. The commandant I think was highly regarded personally by the president."[41] When asked why, Hayes replied, "That's a matter between themselves! (laughs) They were two entirely dissimilar personalities, but apparently they had a high mutual regard for each other. . . . This did not extend to some of Mr. Kennedy's entourage. I think Gen. Shoup had a very good personal working relationship with Mr. McNamara, but this again did not extend to some of the people Mr. McNamara brought in."[42]

Shoup also maintained good relations with Congress. On one occasion, Shoup was able to capitalize on congressional friends to protect the Corps. In 1961, Senator Strom Thurmond criticized the Corps for not training troops on the evils of communism. Shoup resented the criticism but acquiesced when the senator demanded that his staff be allowed to test the average marine's knowledge of marxism. When Thurmond learned that some marines did poorly on the test, he told the press that the Marines were not teaching the dangers of communism. Shoup was incensed by the charge. He counterattacked publicly and found friends in Congress. He remembered that "I didn't feel that we needed to have Strom Thurmond and his henchmen determine for me what I taught the Marines about communism or what the general position of the individual private was, and the fact that he couldn't define dialectical materialism or something like that shouldn't really determine whether he was a good Marine or whether he wasn't, or whether he could fight for his country or whether he couldn't, and to worry people with things of that kind was really immaterial. I thought it was rather ridiculous. So I went to the Secretary of the Navy."[43] The secretary sympathized with Shoup, as did Senators Paul Douglas and Mike Mansfield, and the investigation was dropped.

Complicating the implementation of any defense policy was the simultaneous pressure of events in Southeast Asia, Europe, and Latin America. While the Bay of Pigs operation was being planned, the administration had to consider the deteriorating situation in Laos. By the end of February 1961, communist-backed insurgents had solidified their hold of the Plain of Jars in central Laos. It was feared that if Laos became communist, it could dominate the Mekong lowlands and threaten South Vietnam, Cambodia, and Thailand. The situation precipitated a vigorous debate among the Chiefs, who struggled to find a response that would limit the communist advance without falling into the quagmire of a military stalemate or resorting to a nuclear holocaust. Shoup remarked on "the impropriety and impracticability of logistic support for an operation which was cut off from the sea, and that if anything got going there at all, it might flare into such a sized operation that we just couldn't logistically support. No one, I don't believe, was very much in favor of doing anything except finding some way to stop it and get out. Particularly, we had Marines in the north at the airfield. They played the role that they were expected to play, and I guess it was kind of a bluff that we'd put more troops in [if] we needed them."[44]

Not everyone agreed with Shoup. Some wanted to use nuclear weapons. On that point Shoup was emphatic: "Well, I'll tell you my strong belief. Whoever said that, or whoever even thought that nuclear weapons should be used in Laos was very misinformed about what a proper target for a nuclear weapon consisted of . . . because in all the analysis that I remember, there was never any target presented."[45]

Apparently Shoup's views made an impact. He recalled, "Much later I was told by Mr. Rostow and some other people there that I had the best thought-out idea that came in. I think that's why some of those people over there began to say, 'Well, who the hell is this Marine?'"[46] His reputation for sound thinking on Southeast Asian strategy was established; later it would prove useful when attention shifted to South Vietnam.

Fortunately, no military response was necessary. The crisis in Laos was solved diplomatically when Britain and France cosponsored a Geneva Conference. With U.S. participation, it was agreed to neutralize Laos. Thereafter, events in Southeast Asia temporarily receded into the background.

Moving to the foreground in 1961 was increasing tension with the Soviet Union. Reeling from the Bay of Pigs embarrassment, Kennedy sought to redeem himself. He believed his opportunity came when he met with the Soviet leader Nikita Khrushchev at a summit meeting in Vienna to discuss the division of Germany and Berlin, Laos, and a nuclear test ban treaty. No progress was made on any issues discussed, and Kennedy left the meeting angry with the Soviet leader and convinced that the United States must show its resolve. Shortly after the meeting, Kennedy asked Congress to increase the defense budget and began talking of the need to be prepared to fight. In July, he called up the reserves to respond to any Soviet attempt to block American access to Berlin. The United States and the Soviet Union were now at sword points, and any confrontation might precipitate war.

The following year, the two countries approached the abyss during a crisis over the presence of Soviet missiles in Cuba. The crisis resulted in part from the repeated U.S. attempts to oust Castro. These efforts included an elaborate clandestine program, Operation Mongoose, which Kennedy authorized on November 30, 1961. Under CIA direction, the operation included a variety of schemes to both help the Cubans overthrow Castro or assassinate him and allow U.S. military intervention. When the Joint Chiefs discussed how to use force to support the operation, Shoup cautioned the Chiefs that an invasion of Cuba was a major undertaking. He illustrated his point with an overhead projector. He placed a transparency map of Cuba over a map of the United States to demonstrate that Cuba was not small but eight hundred miles long and stretched over an area that extended from Florida to Chicago. Then he placed a transparency with a red dot on top of the map of Cuba. The dot represented the island of Tarawa, the scene of the bloody battle that led to his receiving the Medal of Honor. He reminded the Joint Chiefs that it took three days and eighteen thousand marines to take the island. He left to their imagination how many more soldiers it would require to subdue Cuba.[47]

Shoup also feared that an invasion of Cuba might involve bombing civilians. Earlier, on May 6, 1961, he had sent a memorandum to the Joint Chiefs questioning whether Cuba should be considered a member of the Sino-Soviet Bloc for targeting purposes under the National Strategic Targeting and Attack policy. Shoup objected to the

policy because it allowed indiscriminate bombing of population cen-
ters in the communist bloc. Shoup went on record expressing his
"opinion [that] this type of attack, if carried out, becomes a questionable and almost immoral act, unworthy of the peoples of the United
States."[48]

All these plans became secondary when, on October 16, intelligence reports of the previous two days revealed that Soviet medium-
range and intermediate-range ballistic missiles were on the ground in
Cuba. The next day, Kennedy's advisers and the Joint Chiefs met sep-
arately to consider the appropriate response. At the meeting of the
Joint Chiefs, they discussed a variety of responses, but they were in
emphatic agreement on two points: first, they opposed limiting air
strikes to the missile sites and, second, if a blockade was installed, it
should serve to enhance, not replace, an air attack. Two days later
they had an opportunity to share their ideas with the president.

Kennedy made it clear to the Chiefs that he feared, "if we attack
Cuban missiles, or Cuba, in any way, it gives them [the Soviets] a clear
line to take Berlin"[49] General Curtis LeMay disagreed: "I don't share
your view that if we knock off Cuba, they're going to knock off Berlin.
We've got the Berlin problem staring us in the face anyway. If we
don't do anything to Cuba, then they're going to push on Berlin and
push *real* hard because they've got us *on the run*." He went on to say,
"So I see no other solution. This blockade and political action I see
leading into war. I don't see any other solution. It will lead right into
war."[50] Admiral George W. Anderson and General Earle G. Wheeler
agreed with LeMay.

Shoup agreed with the Chiefs, and he emphasized the importance
of taking prompt action. He reasoned that "they can damage us increasingly every day. And each day that they increase, we have to
have a more sizable force tied to this problem . . . if we want to eliminate this threat that is now closer. Then we're going to have to go in
there and do it as a full time job to eliminate the threat against us. . . .
And if that decision is made, we must go in with plenty of insurance
of a decisive success in as quick [a time] as possible."[51]

At one point in the discussion, Shoup disagreed with Taylor, who
was now chief of staff. While Taylor concurred that "we can never talk
about invading again, after they get these missiles, because they got
the gun pointed at our head,"[52] he did not share Shoup's view that defending the American naval base at Guantánamo was crucial. Shoup
believed that any U.S. initiative would encourage the Cubans and
Russians to attack Guantánamo, which was vulnerable to surface-to-
surface missile attacks and was within range of Cuban gun emplace-

ments.[53] Something, Shoup argued, had to be done to neutralize that threat. Taylor demurred. He viewed Guantánamo as a liability that was "going to cease to be a useful naval base [and] become more a fortress that's more or less in a permanent state of siege."[54]

Overall, however, there was consensus among the Chiefs that decisive action must be taken immediately. As the meeting was breaking up, three officers remained—Shoup, LeMay, and Wheeler. They exchanged some thoughts on their meeting with Kennedy, and Shoup complimented LeMay on the way he had handled Kennedy. Shoup liked the way LeMay argued that you cannot use a piecemeal approach when you attack Cuba and limit the strike to the missile sites. Like LeMay, Shoup believed, "If the response is limited, you're screwed, screwed, screwed . . . either do the son of a bitch and do it right, and quit friggin' around. You can't fuck around and take a missile out . . . you got to go in and take out the goddamn thing that's going to stop you from doing your job."[55]

Whatever the views of the Joint Chiefs, Kennedy's meeting with them was largely perfunctory or a way of testing his ideas. Before his October 19 meeting with the Joint Chiefs, he established a select

Figure 6.1.   General David M. Shoup sits on sandbags as he talks with Marine Corps PFC William M. James of Lewisburg, Tennessee, at a defensive position on Suicide Ridge at Guantánamo Naval Base. *Source:* © AP / Wide World Photos.

group of advisers to deal with the crisis. The group was designated
the Executive Committee of the National Security Council (Ex Comm)
and included only one member of the Joint Chiefs, the new chairman,
General Taylor. Although the Ex Comm shared the view of the Joint
Chiefs of the necessity of an air attack on the missile sites, it was ruled
out as a first response. Alternatively, they recommended a blockade,
which they labeled a "quarantine." But Kennedy recognized that ultimately the blockade would not work, which left only two options,
trade or invade.

Fortunately, the first option was chosen. Secret negotiations between Robert Kennedy and Soviet Ambassador Anatoly Dobrynin led
to the attorney general's offer to remove missiles in Turkey as part of
a crisis settlement, but without any formal quid pro quo. Additional
steps were taken under the president's orders to encourage the Russians to accept the deal. And on October 28, Khrushchev broadcast his
answer from Moscow. He announced that he had ordered the cessa-
tion of further missile construction and the dismantling of assembled
weapons.

The crisis was over, but Shoup faced another Caribbean problem.
In February 1963, a Marine Corps officer assigned to Haiti on a training mission, Colonel Robert D. Heinl, was expelled from the country.
The Haitian government demanded his departure because Heinl was
an outspoken critic of the regime. Much of his criticism was justified.
He found himself in a poverty-stricken country run by a brutally corrupt leader, François (Papa Doc) Duvalier, who controlled his people
by exploiting their belief in voodoo and intimidating them with a
government of thugs, the infamous Tonton Macoute, and the equally
notorious Milice Civile, his private army.

Duvalier had requested that United States Marines train the Haitian army, but he was unprepared for an officer like Heinl, whose skills
proved too threatening. Under Heinl's command, the most promising
officers were sent to the United States for additional training. Those
who remained were transformed into an effective military force. That
displeased Duvalier, who proceeded to undermine Heinl's progress
by firing the newly trained officers and closing the cadet school.

Heinl was at fault too. From the outset, he revealed his disdain for
the Haitian government and army. Just months after he arrived in November 1959, he leaked to an American magazine the deplorable state
of the Haitian army. The Haitian army chief of staff, who became one
of Heinl's major adversaries, discovered this indiscretion.

Heinl's relations with Haitian authorities continued to deteriorate
until 1962, when they reached crisis proportions. The occasion was

the arrest of Heinl's twelve-year-old son for allegedly making disre-spectful remarks on a public bus. For that offense he was incarcerated in the presidential palace until his friend, Duvalier's son, interceded on his behalf and secured his release. Colonel Heinl exploded and vented his indignation in an accusatory letter to the Haitian govern-ment. Duvalier responded by asking for his removal.

Shortly after Heinl returned to the United States in the spring of 1963, he wrote a two-thousand-word article for *Life* magazine criticiz-ing the Duvalier government, but it was censored by the Defense De-partment. Apparently, the magazine did not secure appropriate clear-ance, and Heinl was implicated in the procedural violation as well. He was summoned to appear before a panel of inquiry to explain his actions. He was charged with violation of a Navy Department regu-lation that stipulated that officers were obligated to submit their man-uscripts for prepublication review. During the hearing, officials from *Life* testified that a Navy information officer gave Heinl verbal per-mission to write the article but not permission to publish it. The board concluded that regulations had in fact been violated but not intention-ally. Shoup's reaction to the panel's findings was to limit his disci-pline to "chewing out" Heinl and not to order a court martial. Subse-quently, Heinl was passed over for promotion to brigadier general. He paid dearly for his indiscretion.

Heinl's indiscretions were minor distractions for Shoup in 1962 and early 1963, because his attention was drawn to the more impor-tant issues of a limited nuclear test ban treaty and a growing Ameri-can military presence in Vietnam. The test ban idea was the Kennedy administration's response to pressure from the scientific community and the public to end atmospheric testing of nuclear weapons. Both the Soviet Union and the United States exploded hydrogen bombs in 1961 and 1962, and by 1963, there was widespread concern over the dangers of radiation fallout from these tests. Kennedy was convinced that underground testing was a satisfactory alternative to atmos-pheric testing, and he used a commencement address at American University on June 10, 1963, to announce his intention to end above-ground testing and invite the Soviet Union to do the same. Kennedy did not, however, want to jeopardize the country's security, which prompted him to ask the Joint Chiefs of Staff for their views on a test ban treaty.

His request for guidance precipitated an intense debate among the Chiefs that became so heated that Taylor directed each to meet pri-vately with Kennedy. Shoup was excluded. Puzzled by his absence, Kennedy invited Shoup to meet with him as well. By that time, the two had developed a close personal relationship. On a number of occasions the president invited his favorite general for late-night White House consultations.[56] Kennedy told Shoup, "I've been looking for you,"[57] and he wondered why he was not included in the schedule of private interviews with the Chiefs. Shoup replied, "You know, Mr. President, I'm only a member, or get to participate in the manner of a member, on matters pertaining to the Marine Corps."[58] Kennedy caught the drift of Shoup's comment and smiled knowingly. He knew the delicacy of Shoup's position but wanted to hear what the commandant had to say. Shoup reminded Kennedy that he had a "responsibility to posterity, [and] had to do everything he could to get a test ban treaty."[59] Kennedy agreed. On October 7, he signed the treaty.

During 1962 and 1963, the other compelling issue that absorbed Shoup's attention was the growing American military involvement in Vietnam. By mid-1962, the American Military Assistance Command force in Vietnam had reached twelve thousand troops. Their mission as advisers was an expression of a seemingly new military doctrine, counterinsurgency. In the Marine Corps, the resident expert on counterinsurgency was not Shoup but one of his subordinates, Major General Victor H. Krulak.

Krulak was appointed to serve the Joint Chiefs of Staff as the Special Assistant for Counterinsurgency and Special Activities. In that capacity he understood his assignment to embrace the idea that "our soldiers were ill-prepared for a war where you weren't going to capture anything. [And] that we needed to re-orient our thinking in terms of how you win a battle which is inside a man's bosom."[60] Why Krulak was chosen is unclear. He heard three different stories: "My acquaintance with the President went back to World War II when he was a PT boat commander. When I got to Washington, he told me that he had selected me personally. General Shoup told me that he had selected me. [And] an admiral who knew me very well told me that he had suggested my name."[61] In any event, Shoup was in favor of Krulak's appointment but dubious about counterinsurgency.

Shoup thought, "Counterinsurgency is an attention-getting word these days," but it was nothing new to marines, who had considerable experience fighting guerrillas.[62] Counterguerrilla warfare was based on small-unit operations, the kind of combat marines were trained for, and Shoup did not believe any additional training was necessary. But he was obliged to follow the orders and prepare marines in counterinsurgency. With some reluctance, he increased training in counterguerrilla warfare and provided instruction in counterinsurgency, but he did nothing to train marines in winning the hearts and minds of a people. With the exception of Krulak, most of the general officers in the Corps shared Shoup's skepticism.

Nevertheless, in time counterinsurgency became the military doctrine for Vietnam. That was not apparent at first as Kennedy struggled to find an appropriate response to the civil war there. His task was difficult because reports from cabinet, congressional, and military observers were often contradictory. After McNamara visited Vietnam for three days, he told reporters, "I've seen nothing but progress and hopeful indications of further progress in the future."[63] Later that year, in December 1962, Mike Mansfield and three other senators toured Vietnam and found the opposite to be true. They believed that Vietnam leader Ngo Dinh Diem was unable to deal with the crisis, and that American aid would be needed for years. Shoup also visited Vietnam in 1962, and he returned convinced that "there was no doubt about it that the position taken by . . . every responsible military man and two Presidents that I admire was that we should not, under any circumstances, get involved in a land warfare in Southeast Asia."[64]

Conditions worsened in Vietnam in 1963, when the Buddhist rebellion there revealed that Diem no longer had the confidence of his people. McNamara's reaction was to advise Kennedy to send General Krulak to Vietnam on a fact-finding mission. Kennedy agreed but insisted that a representative from the State Department be sent as well. In September, Krulak was accompanied by Joseph Mendenhall, the deputy director of the office of Southeast Asia in the State Department. When they returned on September 10, they presented entirely different views: Krulak assured Kennedy that Diem was winning; Mendenhall countered that anarchy and terror reigned in Vietnam. Startled by their conflicting reports, Kennedy asked, "The two of you did visit the same country, didn't you?"[65]

Ultimately Kennedy decided to increase the American military commitment to Vietnam. Shoup was unhappy with that decision but was obliged to follow the orders of the commander in chief. He complied by sending a helicopter squadron and supporting troops to help the South Vietnamese forces achieve more air mobility. The Marine contribution to the war effort coincided with the Army's provision of helicopter transport to the South Vietnamese troops who were attacking Viet Cong guerrillas in the Mekong delta. When helicopters were destroyed by Viet Cong ground fire, members of Congress grew alarmed and investigated. The House Subcommittee on Appropriations held hearings, and Shoup was called to testify. Shoup told the subcommittee that helicopters were essential "considering the terrain

Figure 6.2. Meeting the Mountain People: General David M. Shoup shakes hands with Montagnard mountain tribal chief Yu during a visit to the highlands of central Vietnam. Shoup arrived in Saigon for a four-day inspection tour. *Source:* © AP / Wide World Photos.

and the tactics . . . [and] an envelopment from overhead . . . is the only way they're really going to catch these people."[66]

Shoup began to express his objections when Kennedy expanded the advisory role of the U.S. troops in South Vietnam. On one occasion, Shoup vented his ire to an action officer, Colonel Edwin H. Simmons. Simmons had been negotiating with his counterparts in other services to expand the Marine Corps' share of the military effort in Vietnam. Thinking he had won a significant victory, Simmons reported to Shoup that he had won a generous share for the Marines, which would be allotted fifty to sixty officers and a like number of NCOs to train Vietnamese troops. Shoup asked, "Simmons, what makes you think that I want to put any more marines into Vietnam?" Simmons answered that he thought it would be like the on-the-job training instituted when he commanded the Third Marine Division in Okinawa in 1959. Shoup cut him short with the comment, "We don't want to piss away our resources in that rat hole." The number of Marine advisers in Vietnam remained limited while Shoup was commandant.

Figure 6.3. John Kennedy Jr., nearly three years old, gets smiles from his father, the president, General Shoup, and other military men as they march away from Arlington National Cemetery amphitheater after Veterans Day ceremonies. *Source:* © AP / Wide World Photos.

It is unclear to what degree Shoup's attitude toward Vietnam influenced Kennedy, but Kennedy's private secretary, Evelyn Jones, recalled that Shoup's advice was decisive in 1963. Brigadier General John H. Masters, Shoup's liaison officer for legislative matters, recalls that "Shoup got very thick with President Kennedy on a personal basis, and President Kennedy used to send little notes over there [to Headquarters]. You know, Shoup was very proud of this and he'd call [and say] I forgot my glasses. Can you read who this is from?"[67] In any event, Kennedy began expressing reservations about Vietnam publicly in September 1963, saying that the government was out of touch with the Vietnamese people. It was their war to win. A month later, he told Senator Wayne Morse of Oregon that he was planning to withdraw all advisers by March 19. How firm those plans were is unknown, and an assassin's bullet left that decision to his successor.

Shoup's tour as commandant was almost over when Kennedy was assassinated. Had Kennedy lived, Shoup probably would have served the administration in some capacity. Rumors were already being circulated in Washington newspapers that Shoup might head the

CIA or be the next military adviser to the president. Clearly Kennedy liked Shoup and wanted him to remain. When Shoup's term was ending, Kennedy asked him to serve another tour as commandant. Shoup refused, saying, "If I did so I would prevent ten or eleven other general officers with varying years of service from ever being considered for the job."[68] But Kennedy wanted Shoup to work for him. At a news conference in October 1963, he was asked, "Mr. President, do you expect to use Shoup's service in the Government after he leaves?" The president responded, "I would hope so—if he will—and I would like to have him stay."[69] Any thoughts Shoup might have of staying on ended with Kennedy's death.

Notes

1. Gaddis, *Strategies of Containment*, chapter 7.
2. Geoffrey Perret, *Jack: A Life Like No Other* (New York, 2001), 289.
3. Paramilitary Study Group (hereafter cited as Taylor Report), N.S.F. Collection, John F. Kennedy Library, 3–4.
4. Quoted in J. Hawkins's *Clandestine Services Historical Paper No. 105: Record of Paramilitary Action against the Castro Government of Cuba, 17 March 1960–May 1961*, U.S.M.C. Archives, Marine Corps Combat Development Command, Quantico, Va., 5.
5. Peter Kornbluh, *Bay of Pigs Declassified: The Secret CIA Report on the Invasion of Cuba* (New York, 1998), 274.
6. Piero Gleijes, "Ships in the Night: The CIA, the White House and the Bay of Pigs," *Journal of Latin American Studies* (February 1995), 24–25.
7. Kornbluh, *Bay of Pigs*, 259.
8. Gleijes, "Ships in the Night,"11.
9. Kornbluh, *Bay of Pigs*, 287.
10. Kornbluh, *Bay of Pigs*, 260.
11. Kornbluh, *Bay of Pigs*, 263.
12. Kornbluh, *Bay of Pigs*, 263.
13. Kornbluh, *Bay of Pigs*, 297.
14. Arthur Schlesinger Jr., *A Thousand Days: John F. Kennedy in the White House* (Boston, 1965), 235.
15. Schlesinger, *Thousand Days*, 236.
16. Kornbluh, *Bay of Pigs*, 303; Richard Bissell, *Reflections of a Cold Warrior* (Princeton, N.J., 1996), 183.
17. Bissell, *Reflections*, 184.
18. Hawkins, *Clandestine Services*, H.Q.M.C., 33.
19. Joseph E. O'Connor, Oral History Interview with David M. Shoup, Arlington, Virginia, April 7, 1967, for the John F. Kennedy Library, 16.
20. Taylor Report, 7.
21. Taylor Report, 8.
22. Taylor Report, 11.
23. Taylor Report, 11.
24. Taylor Report, 13.
25. Taylor Report, 17.

26. Taylor Report, 3.

27. Taylor Report, 6.

28. Taylor Report, 10.

29. Taylor Report, 14.

30. Taylor Report, 14.

31. O'Connor, Oral History Interview, 20.

32. O'Connor, Oral History Interview, 21.

33. O'Connor, Oral History Interview, 19.

34. O'Connor, Oral History Interview, 22.

35. H. R. McMaster, *Dereliction of Duty: Lyndon Johnson, Robert McNamara, the Joint Chiefs, and the Lies That Led to Vietnam* (New York, 1997), 9.

36. Maxwell Taylor, *The Uncertain Trumpet* (New York, 1959).

37. Taylor, *Uncertain Trumpet*, 6–7.

38. Frederick L. Weiseman and Edwin Simmons, interview with the author, May 22, 1980.

39. The President's Committee on Equal Opportunity in the Armed Forces, "Equality of Treatment and Opportunity for Negro Military Personnel Stationed within the United States" (Washington, D.C.: Government Printing Office, June 18, 1963), 18.

40. Senate Committee on Armed Services, *Hearings on HR4328: Reassigning US Marine Corps Supply-Duty-Only Officers*, 87th Congress, 1st Session (Washington, D.C., 1961), 5, 6, 19.

41. Oral History Transcript, Lieutenant General Charles H. Hayes, History and Museums Division, H.Q.M.C., p. 221.

42. Oral History Transcript, Hayes, 221.

43. David M. Shoup transcript, "Eisenhower Administration," Columbia Oral History, 33.

44. O'Connor, Oral History Interview, 10.

45. O'Connor, Oral History Interview, 12.

46. O'Connor, Oral History Interview, 10.

47. David Halberstam, *The Best and the Brightest* (New York, 1969), 66; General Edwin H. Simmons, interview with the author, February 27, 1980, Washington, D.C.

48. Memorandum for the Record, May 6, 1961, Shoup MS collection, Hoover Institution on War, Peace, and Revolution, Palo Alto, California.

49. Ernest R. May and Philip D. Zelikow, *The Kennedy Tapes: Inside the White House during the Cuban Missile Crisis* (Cambridge, Mass., 1997), 175.

50. May and Zelikow, *Kennedy Tapes*, 178.

51. May and Zelikow, *Kennedy Tapes*, 182.

52. May and Zelikow, *Kennedy Tapes*, 184.

53. May and Zelikow, *Kennedy Tapes*, 184.

54. May and Zelikow, *Kennedy Tapes*, 183.

55. May and Zelikow, *Kennedy Tapes*, 188.

56. General John H. Masters, interview with the author, August 17, 1980.

57. O'Connor, Oral History Interview, 37.

58. O'Connor, Oral History Interview, 37–41.

59. O'Connor, Oral History Interview, 37.

60. Howard Jablon, "General David M. Shoup, U.S.M.C.: Warrior and War Protester," *Journal of Military History* 60 (July 1996), 525.

61. Jablon, "General David M. Shoup," 525.

62. Millett, *Semper Fidelis*, 548.

63. A. J. Langguth, *Our Vietnam: The War, 1954–1975* (New York, 2000), 176.

64. O'Connor, Oral History Interview, 35.
65. Langguth, *Our Vietnam*, 241.
66. Jablon, "General David M. Shoup," 527.
67. Masters interview.
68. O'Connor, Oral History Interview, 41.
69. *Congressional Quarterly Weekly Report 45* (November 8, 1963), 1922.

7

Rathole

Shoup left the Marine Corps at the end of December 1963, when Lyndon Johnson had announced that he would continue Kennedy's foreign policy in Southeast Asia and elsewhere. Johnson quickly overcame his disdain for Kennedy's advisers on national security and retained many of them. He sought their advice, leaning heavily on the counsel of McNamara until the secretary quit in 1968. After just three days in office, Johnson signed National Security Action Memorandum 273, which specified the security objective in Vietnam as being the prevention of a communist takeover. In December, he approved Operational Plan 34-A to conduct operations against North Vietnam. These two documents set in motion what was to become the military and political disaster of the Vietnam War. Johnson did not want to go down as the president who lost Vietnam. In the end, he lost the presidency.

From the start of LBJ's tenure in office, it was clear that the South Vietnamese government was losing the civil war. When he approved Oplan 34-A in December, he also sent McNamara, McCone, and William Bundy to Vietnam to observe the war. McNamara prepared a gloomy report that predicted that within months a communist takeover was likely. One solution, it was thought, was to replace the ineffective Minh government in South Vietnam. To that end, in January 1964, the administration supported General Nguyen Khanh's coup. But the new government was no more effective than its predecessors. By May, it appeared to Johnson that the United States might be headed for another Korea. His observation turned out to be prophetic. Johnson's immediate concern, however, was political. With an upcoming presidential election in the fall, he had to counter the attack of conservative Republican Senator Barry Goldwater, who accused the administration of being weak and urged attacking North Vietnam.

During the summer of 1964, the United States Navy escorted South Vietnamese patrol boats as they sailed into North Vietnamese territorial waters. In retaliation, North Vietnamese torpedo boats attacked the navy destroyer *Maddox* on August 2, in the Gulf of Tonkin, causing slight damage. Two days later another destroyer, the *C Turner Joy*, reported being attacked but offered no concrete evidence. Nevertheless, on the basis of one verifiable but inconsequential attack and another suspicious act, Johnson accused the North Vietnamese of aggression. He used the incidents as a pretext for asking Congress to authorize military action in Vietnam without a declaration of war. Congress complied on August 7, almost unanimously granting the president the power to "take all necessary measures to repel armed attack against the forces of the United States and to prevent further aggression."[1] The resolution became the legal justification for war under two presidents, Johnson and Nixon.

Johnson's popularity soared after the Tonkin Resolution. Compared with his opponent in the election campaign of 1964, Barry Goldwater, Johnson appeared rational. The Democrats vilified Goldwater as an irresponsible warmonger who would use nuclear weapons and risk a war with China and the Soviet Union. Most of the electorate chose Johnson because they thought he would avoid a wider war in Asia.

But the war continued, and while it grew no wider under Johnson, the American commitment in Vietnam deepened. Within months of the election, Viet Cong guerrillas attacked an American air base at Pleiku on February 7, 1965, and Johnson retaliated with Operation Rolling Thunder, the continuous bombing of North Vietnam. Ground troops were also sent to augment the air war. On March 8, two Marine battalions landed to defend the Da Nang airfield. More troops followed, and by the end of the year almost two hundred thousand American soldiers were fighting in Vietnam.

The escalating war displeased some members of Johnson's administration. Undersecretary of State George W. Ball urged Johnson to cut American losses and leave Vietnam. He was ignored, and Johnson accepted the advice of McNamara, who favored a strategy of applying incremental punishment to dissuade the Viet Cong and North Vietnamese. He took pride in his commanding wartime role and embraced what critics called "McNamara's War."[2]

Johnson was less pleased. He saw the war in Asia as distracting attention from his domestic reform program to expand civil rights and diminish poverty in his Great Society legislative program. So he sought to negotiate with the North Vietnamese and halted the bombing campaign in December 1965. The overture was rebuffed and bombing resumed.

He did not abandon all hope of finding a peaceful solution to the Vietnam conflict and made another offer to North Vietnam in April 1965. In an address at Johns Hopkins University, he promised massive aid to redevelop the Mekong delta, a virtual T.V.A. for North Vietnam, if it would withdraw their troops from South Vietnam. Once again the North Vietnamese refused to negotiate until the United States withdrew. Bribery failed.

Many Americans believed nothing would work. At colleges and universities across the country, faculty and students staged teach-ins to protest the war in Vietnam. Starting at the University of Michigan in March 1965, the campus war protest movement soon spread throughout the country. Shoup joined those protesters on May 14, 1966, when he addressed a world affairs conference at Pierce College in the Los Angeles area. Speaking before an audience of students and professors, he criticized the United States involvement in Vietnam. He told them, "I don't think the whole of Southeast Asia, as related to the present and future safety and freedom of the people of this country, is worth the life or limb of a single American [and] I believe that if we had and would keep our dirty bloody dollar crooked fingers out of the business of these nations so full of depressed exploited people, they will arrive at a solution of their own they design and want, that they fight and work for. And if, unfortunately, their revolution must be of the violent type . . . at least what they get will be their own and not the American style, which they don't want . . . crammed down their throat."[3] Shoup went on to say that he did not believe that the administration ever demonstrated that American interests were threatened by developments in Vietnam. And he asked the audience rhetorically, "Have you read or been instructed about the timetable of disaster for this . . . if we hadn't done and weren't doing what we are in Southeast Asia today? I haven't."[4]

With this speech, Shoup closed ranks with a growing number of other military leaders who opposed the Vietnam War, including Army Generals Matthew B. Ridgway, James Gavin, and Robert L. Hughes; Marine Generals Hugh Hester and Samuel G. Griffith; Rear Admiral Arnold True; and Marine colonels William Carson and James Donovan. They offered testimony, appeared in interviews, and wrote books and articles against the war. Shoup participated in all of these activities. He appeared before the Senate Foreign Relations Committee, the

Figure 7.1.   General David M. Shoup, retired Marine Corps commandant, makes his point during World Affairs Day at Pierce College, May 1966. *Source:* Pierce College *Roundup.*

press interviewed him, and he coauthored an article with Colonel Donovan on interservice rivalry and the escalation of the American military presence in Vietnam. Like the other protesting officers, he added military expertise to the chorus of war protest.[5]

Shoup's outspoken attack was preceded by General Gavin's criticism of the war effort before the Senate Committee on Foreign Relations. On February 8, 1966, Gavin testified that the United States should limit its presence in Vietnam to strong defensible positions in South

Vietnam, "enclaves," and limit troop levels to the current 250,000. Any increase in troops was unnecessary and would be a distraction. Gavin argued that we must "do the best we can with the forces we have deployed to Vietnam, keeping in mind the true meaning of strategy in global affairs."[6]

Two months later, in the April 5 issue of *Look* magazine, General Ridgway published his views in an article entitled, "Pull-out, All-out, or Stand Fast."[7] There he argued that "we should emphatically reject the two extreme courses—'Pull-out or All-out war'—that have been advocated by certain groups."[8] He questioned the underlying rationale of the commitment, the so-called domino effect. It was "a theory I have never accepted."[9] He feared, moreover, the danger of a Chinese intervention if the United States remained. Ridgway cautioned, "We should be wary of experts who feel they can correctly interpret Chinese intentions and can predict how they will react to any of ours."[10] It was axiomatic that the United States must not "base military strategy upon our interpretation of enemy intentions."[11]

Long before the escalation of the American war effort in Vietnam, Ridgway had observed the futility of American involvement there. In the spring of 1954, when the Eisenhower administration considered rescuing the besieged French forces at Dien Bien Phu in their Vietnam War, Ridgway opposed the idea. His objections were based on the report of an Army team of experts he sent to Vietnam. The team discovered that "the area was practically devoid of those facilities which modern forces such as ours find essential to the waging of war. Its telecommunications, highways, railways—all the things that make possible the operation of a modern combat force on land—were almost non-existent. Its port facilities and airfields were totally inadequate, and to provide the facilities we would need would require a tremendous engineer and logistical effort. The land was a land of rice paddy and jungle—particularly adapted to the guerrilla-type warfare."[12]

Shoup shared Ridgway's skepticism. His May 14, 1966, speech at Pierce College was the first of several public statements that attracted considerable attention in the press. On another occasion, in a radio interview Shoup ridiculed the Johnson administration's argument that the Vietnam War was vital to American interests. Shoup believed that the administration is "trying to keep the people worried about the Communists crawling up the banks of Pearl Harbor, or crawling up the Palisades, or crawling up the beaches of Los Angeles, which of course is a bunch of pure unadulterated poppycock. . . . It's about 8,000 miles over the water and . . . they won't have enough ships in the next X years, or not enough planes to get over."[13]

Shoup's comments prompted some adverse press coverage. One particularly critical editorial appeared in a Washington, D.C., newspaper, *The Evening Star*, on December 20, 1967. An editor questioned "whether General Shoup has given thought to the comfort that the enemy *will* derive from his statements. And whether he had considered what would be the effect on the fighting Marines in South Vietnam if the comments of the former Commandant of the Corps should come to their attention. Had anyone used 'free speech' to say such things at Tarawa, General Shoup . . . would have let him have it right between the eyes."[14]

Infuriated, Shoup wrote a letter to the editor.

> You state, "It would be interesting to know, however, whether General Shoup has given thought to the comfort the enemy *will* derive from his statements." I wonder on what facts you conclude that "the enemy will derive" comfort from my words.
>
> For you to publish that the enemy will derive comfort is to imply that, in your judgment, I have committed a treasonable act. I am thankful that it is not your right to judge. I am quite ready to have our American Courts vindicate my honor. However, to satisfy your interest in my thought process, I did give serious consideration as to whether or not my words would impart strength and hope to the enemy. With sharp emphasis I determined in the negative. Further your editorial expresses an interest in whether I considered the effect of my comments on our fighting Marines. I did.
>
> If I know Marines, they fight in accordance with their orders and discuss later. Some of the most intelligent and logical discussion of this war that I have heard has been by returned GIs.
>
> Most of the fighting men, I believe, are thankful that they are fighting for a country that really believes in and practices freedom of speech. And I believe that they hope also that Americans can exercise this freedom free from attempts to intimidate them by insinuation and innuendo indicating that they have given comfort to the enemy.
>
> I believe your analogy with Tarawa to be a poor one. I do not dispute your right to speak your mind, as you did not dispute mine. However, did you consider that before Tarawa we had been attacked; that we had declared war; that we were engaged in mortal combat with the armed forces of a major military power; that they had highly trained troops armed with modern weapons; that they had a combatant fleet; that they were equipped with aircraft capable of destroying our sea, air, and ground forces? Obviously this is a different war. Dialogue may prove as helpful as guns.
>
> Finally, Mr. Editor, I don't believe I would have "at Tarawa" nor that I would now "let anyone have it right between the eyes" because of his exercise of free speech.[15]

A few months later, Shoup's exercise of free speech contributed to his notoriety in the press and elsewhere. On February 16, 1968, a *Chicago Tribune* article reported that the communists in Vietnam were using Shoup's May 14, 1966, speech to undermine the morale of American troops.[16] Leaflets started appearing with excerpts from Shoup's speech. When asked to comment on how his remarks were being used, Shoup replied, "As usual, I was misquoted—just as I was misquoted in the press here. . . . What I said was that . . . Southeast Asia isn't worth a single American life. But I added that maybe the people are, and that's what the administration has been saying all along—that we don't want territory there but we are just helping the people there."[17] The reply was dismissed in the article as being insincere. The reporter noted that Shoup was already on record as saying that it was more in American national interest to fight communism in South America than Vietnam.[18]

Shoup, among others, voiced his objections to the Vietnam War in 1966 and 1967, when the American military presence there was increasing dramatically. By the end of 1967, troop strength approached five hundred thousand. While this military support for South Vietnam was increasing, many South Vietnamese were attacking their own government. In March, Buddhist demonstrators immolated themselves in protest against the Saigon regime. These signs of discontent did not dissuade Johnson. He ordered the resumption of bombing North Vietnam, which continued to have no effect on the Viet Cong rebels or on the North Vietnamese.

The failure of the bombing campaign was obvious to key Johnson advisers. In August 1967, McNamara testified that the bombing of North Vietnam was ineffective. A short time later he joined other disillusioned advisers, such as McGeorge Bundy, George Ball, and Bill Moyers, who had left the administration. Outside the administration, members of Congress were also expressing their dissatisfaction with the war. William Fulbright, chairman of the Senate Foreign Relations Committee, joined fellow committeemen Frank Church, Albert Gore Sr., Mike Mansfield, and Wayne Morse in opposing the war. Fulbright's committee invited an array of experts to testify in televised hearings. Their testimony strengthened and publicized arguments against the war.

Shoup was one of the expert witnesses to appear before the committee in March 1968. At that time, the atmosphere in the United States was charged with revulsion toward the war. In January, the North Vietnamese had seized provincial capitals and attacked the American embassy in Saigon. U.S. and South Vietnamese troops had

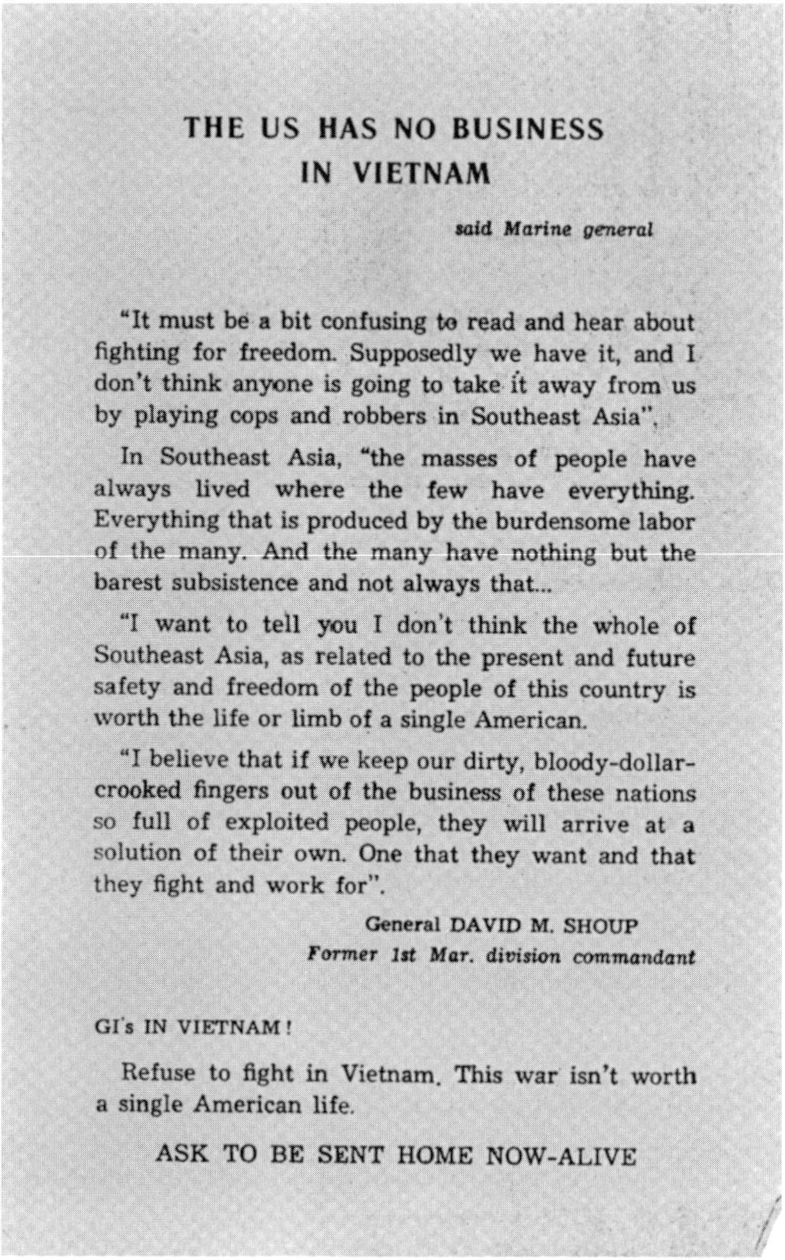

THE US HAS NO BUSINESS
IN VIETNAM

said Marine general

"It must be a bit confusing to read and hear about fighting for freedom. Supposedly we have it, and I don't think anyone is going to take it away from us by playing cops and robbers in Southeast Asia".

In Southeast Asia, "the masses of people have always lived where the few have everything. Everything that is produced by the burdensome labor of the many. And the many have nothing but the barest subsistence and not always that...

"I want to tell you I don't think the whole of Southeast Asia, as related to the present and future safety and freedom of the people of this country is worth the life or limb of a single American.

"I believe that if we keep our dirty, bloody-dollar-crooked fingers out of the business of these nations so full of exploited people, they will arrive at a solution of their own. One that they want and that they fight and work for".

General DAVID M. SHOUP
Former 1st Mar. division commandant

GI's IN VIETNAM!

Refuse to fight in Vietnam. This war isn't worth a single American life.

ASK TO BE SENT HOME NOW-ALIVE

Figure 7.2. North Vietnamese propaganda pamphlet from 1968: "The U.S. has no business in Vietnam," said Marine General David M. Shoup. *Source:* Martin Florian Herz Collection, Hoover Institution Archives.

managed to repulse the offensive, but the victory felt like defeat to many Americans. And Shoup typified the growing antipathy toward the war. He told the Senate Foreign Relations Committee that the loss of Vietnam certainly did not constitute a threat to our security. "It is ludicrous to think," he argued, "that just because we lose in South Vietnam that very soon somebody is going to be crawling and knocking at the doors of Pearl Harbor."[19] He viewed the conflict as a civil war and believed the Vietnamese should be left alone to decide their political destiny. Our objectives appeared questionable to Shoup because it "was not to defeat the Armed Forces of North Vietnam, but rather . . . to rid South Vietnam, of these interlopers, so called, from the north and any others who have developed in the south. . . . this kind of thing limits our actions."[20]

In any event, Shoup did not believe the war could be won, because the North Vietnamese could match the United States man for man in a limited war. If the war were expanded, the Chinese might intervene. Should that happen, the United States would have to use nuclear weapons. Shoup saw withdrawal as the only alternative to the embroilment. Earlier, in 1967, he had suggested that a negotiated settlement was possible if Johnson would invite North and South Vietnam leaders to peace talks. Now Shoup was more skeptical.

The committee asked him if a partial withdrawal might work, and if the Gavin enclave plan had any value. Gavin had testified earlier that the United States could limit its troops to current levels, abandon the jungles and highland, and fortify major cities as defensible enclaves. Shoup disparaged that idea and told the committee, "You can retreat clear down to around Saigon or Danang or any other place all you want to, but you won't be carrying out the objectives that the armed forces have been given."[21] Shoup did not equate holding enclaves with controlling a country.[22]

As Shoup was testifying in March 1968, the political world around Johnson was crumbling. In the Democratic presidential primary in New Hampshire, Senator Eugene McCarthy almost defeated him. At that point, Senator Robert F. Kennedy decided to join the presidential race as an antiwar candidate. Even Johnson's new Secretary of Defense, Clark Clifford, cautioned him the war could not be won. Wherever he turned, Johnson saw defeat. His response was stunning. On March 31, he announced he would not seek reelection and would concentrate on negotiating a settlement in Vietnam. He halted bombing North Vietnam in an attempt to encourage peace negotiations.

Nothing worked for Johnson in 1968. The entire country seemed to totter on the brink of political upheaval. Two assassinations, of

Martin Luther King Jr. on April 4, and Robert Kennedy two months later, unnerved the country. War protests were growing and intensifying. When the Democratic Party met in Chicago in August, where Vice President Hubert Humphrey won the nomination, antiwar demonstrators outside the convention were being hauled off to jail. It was an inauspicious beginning to a doomed campaign.

In November, a rejuvenated Richard Nixon narrowly defeated Humphrey. Before the campaign, Nixon had seemed headed for political obscurity after his 1962 defeat in the California gubernatorial race. His remarkable comeback promised little. Aside from vague assurances to conclude an honorable peace, he offered no concrete proposals for ending the war. It would take him four more years to extricate the country from its military commitment in Vietnam.

Nixon's approach to Vietnam was evident in May 1969, when he met with South Vietnamese president Nguyen Van Thieu at Midway. The meeting marked the beginning of Nixon's policy of "Vietnamization," to reduce American troops so that South Vietnamese soldiers would do more of the fighting. The United States reduced troops from 535,000 to 400,000 within a year. At the same time the air war was intensified and broadened to include sorties into neutral Cambodia, which was being used as a base for North Vietnamese operations. Shortly after the Midway meeting the president announced his Nixon Doctrine, which promised to limit American participation in future wars to material support and military advisers, not combat troops. But the doctrine would not go into effect until after the Vietnam War.

Three months later, national security adviser Henry Kissinger began secret negotiations with North Vietnamese representatives in Paris. Kissinger indicated to them that the United States wanted to leave Vietnam but without appearing weak or to be abandoning an ally. He suggested separating military and political considerations as long as North Vietnam delayed seizing the South. North Vietnamese representative Xuan Thuy was not receptive. The diplomatic process to end the war was just starting.

Attempts to find a dignified exit from Vietnam did not placate the American public. In 1969, the antiwar movement mounted its largest demonstration to date. On the weekend of November 14, almost a half million protesters gathered in Washington. Their presence had no effect on Nixon; he watched a football game on television while protesters rallied against the war. Six months later, Nixon did take notice of opposition to the war when national guardsmen fired on student protesters at Kent State University in Ohio, killing four and injuring twenty-one. Thousands gathered in protest at the Lincoln Memorial in Washington on May 7. This time Nixon talked with the dissidents, but he did not change his policy.

These first tumultuous years of the Nixon administration deeply affected Shoup. It aroused his suspicions that something was fundamentally wrong with the whole process of making national security policy. He blamed the military establishment. Before 1969, much of Shoup's criticism was similar to the objections of other dissenting senior officers, such as Generals Matthew B. Ridgway, James Gavin, and J. Lawton Collins and Admiral Harry D. Felt. All these officers shared the conviction that Vietnam was outside the realm of American national security interests and that a guerrilla war there could not be won while the United States supported a corrupt regime in the south.[23] In particular, Shoup shared Gavin and Ridgway's view of the futility of a massive bombing campaign. Shoup believed that the bombing only served to stiffen North Vietnamese resistance. In any case, it was not working. Supplies still flowed south along the "Ho Chi Minh autobahn."[24]

Shoup went beyond the criticism of the other dissenting generals when he blamed the war on pervasive American militarism and interservice rivalry. His indictment was published in a coauthored article for the *Atlantic Monthly*, "The New American Militarism."[25] Though largely written by his collaborator, Colonel James A. Donovan, it expressed Shoup's long-standing suspicions of what influenced national security decision making. Borrowing from the work of sociologist C. Wright Mills, Shoup and Donovan argued that America had become a militaristic and aggressive society. With industrial support, they averred, the military dominated American life. Preoccupation with strategy, tactics, and doctrine, central to military thinking, became part of the country's cognitive process.

Of greater concern to the authors was the impact of interservice rivalry on the escalation of the war. They charged that a "first to fight" mentality dominated the services. The competition to be the first service to commit troops to combat was, they argued, the driving force behind the increase in troop strength in Vietnam in 1965. The rivalry between Navy–Marine lift forces and Army–Air Force lift forces resulted in jostling for assignments and an excessive emphasis on combat readiness and rapid deployment in the services.[26] As late as 1968, some senior officers who wanted a larger Marine combat role in Vietnam thought the Corps was being slighted and losing the deployment race.[27]

Donovan later expanded the indictment presented in the article in his book *Militarism USA*. Shoup wrote the foreword to the book, in which he summarized his own objections to the war. He repeated what he had said before: "I had opposed the idea that such a small country in that remote part of the world constituted an economic interest or a strategic threat to the welfare of the United States. In the past I have frequently expressed concern about military policies or plans, which would commit American troops to a land war against the oriental peoples of Southeast Asia."[28] Shoup also emphasized in his foreword that "by now it should be clear that the theories of counterinsurgency, graduated response, and limited war are unable to support political commitment and objectives that are not in consonance with the realities of people's revolutions and irregular warfare in Asia . . . there are limits of U.S. power and our capabilities to police the world."[29]

Shoup found the alternative proffered by the Nixon administration, Vietnamization, equally unrealistic. He viewed it as a political device intended to placate the American public that would never end the war.[30] Even a reduction in U.S. troops would still require millions of dollars in aid to help the South Vietnamese stay in the fight. Thus, for Shoup, there was no alternative to a complete military withdrawal from the war.[31]

Other Marine generals, particularly those directing the fighting in Vietnam, were unhappy with the war effort, but they believed that a different strategy would work. Wallace M. Greene Jr., who succeeded Shoup as commandant and served from 1963 to 1967, and Victor H. Krulak, commander of the Fleet Marine Force, Pacific, opposed Westmorland's war of attrition. Their alternatives, counterinsurgency and more air attacks, were ignored by the Johnson and Nixon administrations.

Unlike marines on active duty, Shoup remained an outspoken critic, and many marines did not welcome his public opposition to the war. Some thought his behavior was treasonous. Retired Colonel Robert Heinl attacked Shoup for his dissent. He wrote in one newspaper article that Shoup was going "sour on his country and his brother officers."[32] Heinl may have been settling an old score with Shoup for being disciplined and passed over for promotion. Other marines, even Shoup's closest friends, were upset. General Frederick L. Weiseman thought Shoup was slipping mentally.[33] General Rathvon McC. Tompkins kept a copy of a North Vietnamese propaganda leaflet with a quotation from Shoup's May 1966 antiwar speech as a reminder of his friend's disloyalty. For many years, he did not speak to Shoup. Shoup paid dearly for his dissention. He was alienated from the Corps he loved.

Shoup, like other protesters, apparently did not influence the Nixon administration. In 1971, the revelations of the Pentagon Papers documented what Shoup and other critics had long suspected. Nixon retaliated by having Daniel Ellsberg, the man who made the papers public, investigated to discredit him. The administration continued to reduce troop strength, down to 140,000 by year's end, while Kissinger continued secret negotiations with the North Vietnamese. It would take two more years for the last troops to leave Vietnam and the American war there to end.

What effect the protest of Shoup and others had on the final outcome is moot. In 1973, most antiwar activists believed their cause was a noble failure.[34] Yet the dissenting generals like Shoup could claim some success in promoting the antiwar movement, encouraging media exposure, abetting congressional complaint, and inspiring veteran protest. Some politicians, such as Symington and Fulbright, praised Shoup for providing his expert criticism. Others, including Johnson and Nixon, feared Shoup and had the FBI spy on him. Praised or feared, Shoup added intelligence as well as nobility to the crusade to stop the war.

Notes

1. *Congressional Record*, 110, August 7, 1964.
2. *New York Times*, April 25, 1964.
3. Jablon, "General David M. Shoup," 532.
4. Jablon, "General David M. Shoup."
5. Robert Buzzanco, "The American Military Rationale against the Vietnam War," *Political Science Quarterly* 101, no. 4 (1986): 559–76. See also McMaster, *Dereliction of Duty*.
6. James Deakin, "Big Brass Lambs," *Esquire* 68 (December 1967): 144ff. See also U.S. Congress, Committee on Foreign Relations, Supplemental Foreign Assistance, Fiscal Year 1966—Vietnam, 89th Congress, 2d Session, 1966.
7. Matthew B. Ridgway, "Pull-out, All-out, or Stand Fast," *Look* 30, no. 7 (April 5, 1966): 81–84.
8. Ridgway, "Pull-out," 84.
9. Ridgway, "Pull-out," 82.
10. Ridgway, "Pull-out," 84.
11. Ridgway, "Pull-out," 84.
12. Matthew B. Ridgway, *Soldier: The Memoirs of Matthew B. Ridgway* (New York, 1956), 276–77.
13. *Indianapolis Star*, December 19, 1967.
14. Editorial, *Evening Star*, December 20, 1967.
15. Shoup, letter to editor, *Evening Star*, December 22, 1967.
16. Fred Farrar, *Chicago Tribune Press Service*, February 16, 1968.
17. Farrar, *Chicago Tribune*.
18. Farrar, *Chicago Tribune*.
19. U.S. Senate Committee on Foreign Relations, *Present Situation in Vietnam*, 90th Congress, 2d Session, March 20, 1968, 3.

20. Senate Committee on Foreign Relations, *Present Situation in Vietnam*, 6.

21. Senate Committee on Foreign Relations, *Present Situation in Vietnam*, 16–17.

22. Senate Committee on Foreign Relations, *Present Situation in Vietnam*, 25, 28.

23. Robert Buzzanco, *Masters of War: Military Dissent and Politics in the Vietnam Era* (New York, 1996), 9.

24. Buzzanco, *Masters of War*, 569.

25. David M. Shoup and James A. Donovan, "The New American Militarism," *Atlantic Monthly* 223 (April 1969): 51–56.

26. Jablon, "General David M. Shoup," 533.

27. Jablon, "General David M. Shoup," 534.

28. David M. Shoup, foreword to James A. Donovan, *Militarism U.S.A.* (New York, 1970), xi.

29. Shoup, foreword to Donovan, *Militarism*, xi–xii.

30. Buzzanco, *Masters of War*, 570.

31. Buzzanco, *Masters of War*, 570.

32. *Detroit News*, March 28, 1969, 8A.

33. Frederick L. Weiseman and Edwin Simmons, interview with the author, May 22, 1980.

34. Charles DeBenedetti with Charles Chatfield, *An American Ordeal: The Antiwar Movement of the Vietnam Era* (Syracuse, N.Y., 1990), 355.

8

"Dollar Crooked Fingers"

After American troops withdrew from Vietnam, Shoup, like the proverbial old soldier, faded away. Left without a war to fight or to protest, he turned reflective and started to write his autobiography. He never got very far with the project, only a title and a short outline. But what he wrote was revealing. He saw himself as a very lucky man, fortunate enough to narrowly escape death many times. The title might have served as his choice for an epitaph: "The Cat Has But Nine." Shoup's life was not, however, just a series of fortuitous circumstances. His relentless drive and hardheaded intelligence shaped his destiny to become a professional soldier—the quintessential marine.

His idea of soldiering was simple. Marines were trained to fight, not to win the hearts and minds of people embroiled in a civil war. Shoup stressed combat readiness above all else and often looked askance at military hardware that he believed only served to enrich the weapons industry. He knew the value of technology, as he demonstrated when he used LVTs at Tarawa. Nevertheless, he firmly believed, "You don't overlook the fact that no battle was ever won by Marines in a boat, amphibious tractor, helicopter, ship or transport air craft. Battles are won by Marines with their feet on the ground."[1] Combat readiness necessitated training, and when Shoup became commandant he insisted that all commanders, whatever their level of command, train their troops to fight. That did not include indoctrination in the evils of communism, as he demonstrated when Senator Strom Thurmond criticized the Marine Corps for inadequately educating troops on the perils of communism.

In Shoup's pursuit of combat readiness he was demanding and unforgiving. He was particularly severe with senior officers who, if they failed in any way, were subjected to a "chewing out," usually laced with profanity and sometimes in the presence of subordinates, a serious breach of military decorum. Shoup was equally harsh with mindless conformists. When any officer justified his advice with the comment that it was always done that way, Shoup would cut him short and hand him a copy of the poem "Cow Path." The poem explains how cow paths evolved into modern highways: paths became trails, trails become roads, and roads became highways. It all started without any intelligent planning. Likewise, Shoup remonstrated, only bovine minds followed well-trodden paths. He wanted independent judgment from his officers.

Shoup was a spit-and-polish marine. He expected his troops always to look sharp. On one occasion, when an assistant naval attaché assigned to a Latin American embassy for two years paid a courtesy call on the commandant, he appeared before Shoup wearing dirty and frayed combat ribbons. Shoup yanked the ribbons from his uniform and gave him a severe tongue-lashing. He left those ribbons on his desk for weeks to remind other officers how to dress. Proper attire did not include the swagger stick, which he considered an elitist affectation, and he ridiculed other services that wore berets.

Most of Shoup's time was spent making the Marine Corps into an effective fighting force, and he was less concerned with its relative position within the military establishment. He understood that his selection as commandant was, in part, a rebuke of General Merrill B. Twining and his supporters, who had vigorously defended the Corps during the merger controversy. But Shoup reminded the presidents he served of the unique capabilities of the Corps in amphibious operations. And despite his limited membership on the Joint Chiefs of Staff, he became Kennedy's favorite Chief.[2]

Shoup's influence on national security policy varied. Though he later vehemently denied he supported an invasion of Cuba, Shoup, along with the other Chiefs, advised a full-scale attack. Shoup cautioned his fellow officers that it was a major undertaking by comparing it with the amphibious assault on Tarawa. Like the other Chiefs, he rejected some of the piecemeal alternatives considered by Kennedy's advisers. In any event, Kennedy ignored the Joint Chiefs and ultimately found a diplomatic solution. Shoup's advice had greater impact on other national security issues. His early rejection of extensive force in Laos and his consistent opposition to a military commitment in Vietnam were more persuasive. And Kennedy appreciated his support for the nuclear test ban treaty, which the other Chiefs discouraged.

Sometimes Shoup's advice was difficult to follow. Deputy Secretary of Defense Roswell L. Gilpatric once described Shoup as Delphic because his recommendations were cryptic, though he credited Shoup with being very helpful when the test ban treaty was under consideration. Shoup was not above stretching the truth, as he did when he testified before the Taylor committee on the Bay of Pigs, denying that he had any knowledge of the decision to cancel additional air strikes on D-Day. On one subject, he never dissembled or equivocated—that was his opposition to war in Vietnam.

Much of Shoup's behavior, including his attitude toward war, can be traced to his upbringing. He grew up in rural poverty, which made an indelible impression on him. Throughout his life he was obsessed with money. Even his gambling was indicative of that obsession. During World War II, a fellow officer observed him counting his winnings on his way to another poker game. He asked Shoup why he continued to play. Shoup replied, "It's business, strictly business."[3] Shoup was always calculating what things cost, including warfare. When he joined the Marine Corps in 1927, he saw the film *What Price Glory?* Shoup recorded in his journal: "From the first image upon the screen until the last faded completely into *Finis*, I was completely overcome with the greatness of the picture. It was even more stirring to me than the play as produced in Indianapolis some ten months before—perhaps because I witnessed the picture as a Marine and the play as a college student."[4] Shoup was deeply moved by the unglamorous portrayal of warfare in the play and the film. In one scene, the "Trench of Death," a line of soldiers was buried in earth with only their bayonets exposed. Even more dramatic was the dialogue in the play's second act. The character Lieutenant Moore enters the wine cellar where Americans are resting and cries,

> And since six o'clock there's been a wounded sniper in the tree by that orchard angel crying "Kamerad! Kamerad!" Just like a big crippled whippoorwill. What price glory now? Why in God's name can't we all go home? Who gives a damn for this lousy, stinking little town but the poor French bastards who live here? God damn it! You talk about courage, and all night long you hear a man who's bleeding to death on a tree calling you "Kamerad" and asking you to save him.[5]

As a marine, Shoup had to contemplate that the price of glory might be his life.

On two memorable occasions in his career, he calculated that the price of glory was too high. First, when he was a young lieutenant in China in 1927, he blamed missionaries, businessmen, and diplomats for squandering American military resources in a civil war that was none of our business. Later, in 1966, he protested the war in Vietnam, blaming it on America's militaristic thinking and self-aggrandizing services. The root of both evils was the grasping nature of "our dirty, bloody, dollar crooked fingers" in foreign affairs.[6]

Shoup always worried that business interests and their allies in the military excessively influenced foreign policy. Like Eisenhower, he feared the growing military-industrial complex that was promoting unnecessary weapons technology at an enormous cost to the American people. Politicians were at fault too. Defense contracts and base locations often clouded their judgment. Greed triumphed over national security.

Many of Shoup's attitudes and anxieties can be traced to his upbringing during the Progressive Era, a period when reformers campaigned to rein in the power of big business. It was also a time of intense nationalism that led some progressive leaders, such as Senator Albert Beveridge of Indiana, to champion foreign adventures. The culmination of progressivism at home and abroad was the Wilsonian domestic agenda of transformational reforms and a crusade to "make the world safe for democracy." Shoup seems to have absorbed the progressive antipathy toward big business and the midwestern progressives' aversion to U.S. imperialism.

More than anyone else in his family, he revered his older brother, who served in World War I. Shoup's devotion to his brother and others in his family displays a more fundamental characteristic. He was an intensely emotional man. To many who served with him or under him, he seemed insensitive, a DI in a general's uniform. But Shoup camouflaged his emotions well. Often he confined his deepest expressions of feeling to his poetry. On one occasion, however, he revealed what motivated him. When he was commandant, he was asked to explain why marines had such great esprit. He replied, "Love: love of country, love of the Corps and its traditions, and love of the man to the right and to the left of you."[7] Those feelings of love and loyalty guided him throughout his career. The same passion impelled his dissent during the Vietnam War.

Notes

1. David M. Shoup, *Remarks by Commandant of the Marine Corps to Staff*, January 4, 1960, HQMC, Historical Division, 8–9.

2. Sorenson recalled that Shoup was Kennedy's favorite Chief. Theodore Sorenson, *Kennedy* (New York, 1965), 607.

3. General Rathvon McC. Tompkins, interview with the author, August 17, 1980.

4. Shoup, *Marines in China*, 22.

5. Laurence Stallings and Maxwell Anderson, *What Price Glory?* in *Three American Plays* (New York, 1926), 59.

6. "Remarks by General David M. Shoup, U.S. Marine Corps (Retired) at the 10th Annual Junior College World Affairs Day, Pierce College, Los Angeles, California," *Congressional Record*, Senate, February 20, 1967, 3976.

7. Shoup, *Marines in China*, vii.

Bibliographical Essay

Archival collections are the point of departure for any investigation of Shoup or the Marine Corps. Shoup's papers are located at the Hoover Institution on War, Revolution, and Peace, Stanford, California; there is a David M. Shoup biographical file at the Marine Corps Historical Center, Washington, D.C. The center also houses other manuscript collections central to this study, including the papers of James Donovan, Wallace M. Greene, Jr., and Victor H. Krulak. There are important oral history collections there as well, notably oral histories of Robert H. Cushman, Victor H. Krulak, Thomas Wilkerson, David M. Shoup, and Edwin H. Simmons. Of the published documents that are pertinent, the most important are found in U.S. Department of State, Papers Relating to the Foreign Relations of the United States: Vietnam, Vol. 1 (Washington, D.C., 1961), Vietnam, Vol. 2 (Washington, D.C., 1962), Vietnam Vol. 3 (Washington, D.C., January–August 1963), Vietnam Vol. 4 (Washington, D.C., August–December 1963), and Cuba Vol. 10 (Washington, D.C., 1997).

Any study of a marine or the Corps must start with the encyclopedic work of Allan R. Millett, *Semper Fidelis: The History of the United States Marine Corps* (New York, 1980). Another general work that is useful is David Farber, *The Age of Great Dreams: America in the 1960s* (New York, 1994). Arthur M. Schlesinger Jr., *A Thousand Days* (New York, 1982), is a memoir and defense of the Kennedy years. For the Johnson period, Robert Dallek, *Lone Star Rising: Lyndon Johnson and His Times, 1908–1960* (New York, 1991), is an important biography. The Nixon administrations are carefully chronicled in two books by Stephen Ambrose, Nixon, Vol. 2, *The Triumph of a Politician, 1962–1972* (New York, 1989) and *Nixon: Ruin and Recovery, 1978–1990* (New York, 1992) as well as Jeffrey Kimball's *Nixon's Vietnam War* (Lawrence, Kans., 1998).

For specific works relating to Shoup's early life and what America was like at that time, the first step is reading James H. Madison's *The Indiana Way: A State History* (Bloomington, 1986). Additional

background material is also readily available in various issues of the
Indiana Magazine of History 1 (Bloomington, 1905–).

Since Shoup was born and matured during the progressive era,
the books relating to the foreign policy of that era that should be con-
sulted include Howard K. Beale, *Theodore Roosevelt and the Rise of
America to World Power* (Baltimore, 1956); Walter V. Scholes and Marie
V. Scholes, *The Foreign Policies of the Taft Administration* (Columbia,
Mo., 1970); and Arthur Link, *Woodrow Wilson: A Brief Biography*
(Cleveland, 1963). An excellent account of the connection between
progressivism and imperialism is found in William E. Leuchtenburg,
"The Progressive Movement and American Foreign Policy,
1898–1916," *Mississippi Valley Historical Review* 39, no. 3 (Urbana, Ill.,
December 1952): 483–504.

Valuable accounts of American policy in China when Shoup was
stationed there in the 1920s and 1930s are Akira Iriye, *Across the Pacific: An Inner History of American-East Asian Relations* (New York,
1967); Paul Varg, *Missionaries, Chinese and Diplomats: The American
Protestant Missionary Movement in China, 1890–1952* (Princeton, N.J.,
1958); and Jerry Israel, *Progressivism and the Open Door: America and
China, 1905–1921* (Pittsburgh, 1971). Dorothy Borg's *American Policy
and the Chinese Revolution, 1925–1928* (New York, 1947) remains the
standard work on the subject.

For World War II, the starting point would be David M. Kennedy's
comprehensive narrative, *Freedom from Fear: The American People in Depression and War, 1929–1945* (New York, 1999). Equally important are
three volumes in the World War II series History of U.S. Marine Corps
Operations in World War II, ed. Frank O. Hough, Verle E. Ludwig,
Henry I. Shaw Jr.: Vol. 1, *Pearl Harbor to Guadalcanal,* (Washington,
D.C., 1958); and Vol. 3, ed. Henry I. Shaw Jr., Bernard C. Nalty, and Edwin T. Turnblodh, *Central Pacific Drive* (Washington, D.C., 1966). The
best account to date on the battle of Tarawa is Joseph H. Alexander's
Utmost Savagery: The Three Days of Tarawa (Annapolis, 1995). The latest
edition of Robert Sherrod's *Tarawa: The Story of Battle* (Annapolis, Md.,
1995) remains the classic account.

In the post–World War II period, Shoup remained outside the battle to prevent the merger of the Marine Corps with other services. Victor Krulak's account of that struggle in his book *First to Fight: An Inside View of the Marine Corps* (Annapolis, 1984) contains the Marine
argument. It should be read along with Gordon W. Keiser's *The US
Marine Corps and Defense Unification, 1944–47: The Politics of Survival*
(Washington, D.C., 1982). But Shoup was involved in the Ribbon
Creek tragedy. A complete account of that episode is found in Keith

Fleming, *The U.S. Marine Corps in Crisis: Ribbon Creek and Recruit Training* (Columbia, Mo., 1990).

Since Shoup was named commandant by Eisenhower, an overview of that period is essential. Stephen Ambrose, *Eisenhower: The President* (New York, 1983), remains the basic text. On the Eisenhower-Dulles relationship and foreign policy, useful accounts are Richard H. Immerman, *John Foster Dulles: Piety, Pragmatism, and Power in U.S. Foreign Policy* (Wilmington, Del., 1999), and John Lewis Gaddis, *Strategies of Containment: A Critical Appraisal of Postwar American National Security Policy* (New York, 1982). Policy toward Latin America is reviewed critically in Stephen G. Robe, *Eisenhower and Latin America: The Foreign Policy of Anticommunism* (Chapel Hill, 1988). On Central America the noteworthy works are Walter LaFeber, *Inevitable Revolutions: The United States in Central America* (New York, 1983), and Richard H. Immerman, *The CIA in Guatemala: The Foreign Policy of Intervention* (Austin, 1982). On the war in Vietnam, Lloyd C. Gardner's *Approaching Vietnam: From World War II through Dienbienphu, 1941–1954* (New York, 1988) and David L. Anderson's, *Trapped by Success: The Eisenhower Administration and Vietnam, 1953–1961* (New York, 1991) are important studies.

The Kennedy years are presented objectively in Richard Reeves, *President Kennedy: Profile of Power* (New York, 1993). Essential reading on the Bay of Pigs and Cuban missile crisis are Trumbull Higgins, *The Perfect Failure: Kennedy, Eisenhower, and the CIA at the Bay of Pigs* (New York, 1987), Graham Allison and Philip D. Zelikow, *Essence of Decision: Explaining the Cuban Missile Crisis*, 2d ed. (New York, 1999), and Ernest R. May and Philip D. Zelikow, *The Kennedy Tapes: Inside the White House during the Cuban Missile Crisis* (Cambridge, Mass., 1997).

Material on the Vietnam War and antiwar protests is voluminous. A fine survey of the war is Robert D. Schulzinger, *A Time for War: The United States and Vietnam, 1941–1975* (New York, 1997). Antiwar protesting is ably discussed by Charles DeBenedetti with Charles Chatfreel in *An American Ordeal: The Antiwar Movement of the Vietnam Era* (Syracuse, N.Y., 1990). For senatorial opinion, see Randall Bennett Woods's *Fulbright: A Biography* (New York, 1995). Military objections to the war are analyzed in Robert Buzzanco's thought-provoking *Masters of War: Military Dissent and Politics in the Vietnam Era* (New York, 1996) and H. R. McMaster's *Dereliction of Duty: Lyndon Johnson, Robert McNamara, and the Joint Chiefs of Staff and the Lies that Led to Vietnam* (New York, 1997) is a persuasive critique of strategic blunder.

Bibliography

General

Benis, Frank M. *Marine Corps Oral History Collection Catalog*. 2d ed. Washington, D.C.: History and Museum Division, HQMC, 1979.

Blakeney, Jane. *Heroes: U.S. Marine Corps, 1861–1955*. Washington, D.C.: Jane Blakeney, 1957.

Condit, Kenneth, and Major John H. Johnstone, USMC. *A Brief History of Marine Corps Staff Organization*. Historical Reference Series 25. Washington, D.C.: Historical Branch, HQMC, 1963.

Current Biography. Monthly and annual issues, indexed. New York: H. W. Wilson, 1940–.

Dollen, Charles. *Bibliography of the United States Marine Corps*. New York: Scarecrow Press, 1963.

Facts on File. Weekly, indexed. New York: Facts on File, 1941–.

Guide to the Sources of U.S. Military History. Hamden, Conn.: Archon, 1975.

Harvard Guide to American History. Cambridge, Mass.: Harvard Univ. Press, 1966.

Heinl, Robert D. *Soldiers of the Sea: The United States Marine Corps, 1775–1962*. Annapolis, Md.: U.S. Naval Institute, 1962.

Johnstone, Major John A. *An Annotated Bibliography of the United States Marines in Guerrilla, Anti-Guerrilla, and Small War Actions*. Washington, 1966.

Krulak, Lieutenant General Victor, USMC (Ret.). *First to Fight: An Inside View of the U.S. Marine Corps*. Annapolis, Md.: U.S. Naval Institute, 1984.

Lewis, Charles L. *Famous American Marines*. Boston: L. C. Page, 1950.

Marine Corps Gazette. Quantico, Va.: Marine Corps Association, 1916–.

Marine Corps Officers. Private Papers. Washington, D.C.: Marine Corps Historical Center, Washington Navy Yard.

Millett, Allan R. *Semper Fidelis: The History of the United States Marine Corps*. New York: Macmillan, 1980.

Moran, John B. *Marine's Handbook of Writing about Marines: The Definitive Bibliography of the U.S. Marine Corps*. Chicago: Moran/Andrews, 1971.

Morris, Richard B. *Encyclopedia of American History*. New York: Harper and Row, 1970.

Parker, Captain William D. *A Concise History of the U.S. Marine Corps, 1775–1969*. Washington, D.C.: U.S. Marine Historical Division, 1970.

Plischke, Elmer. *American Foreign Relations: A Bibliography of Official Sources*. College Park: Univ. of Maryland, 1955.

Records of the United States Marine Corps. National Archives, Record Group 127. Washington, D.C., 1970.

Schuon, Karl, comp. *USMC Biographical Dictionary*. New York: Franklin Watts, 1963.

Shaw, Henry J. *The Historical Publications of the U.S. Marine Corps*. In *Official Histories*, ed. Robin D. S. Higham. Manhattan: Kansas State Univ. Library, 1970.

U.S. Department of State. *Foreign Relations of the US* (USFR), annual series. Washington, D.C.: Government Printing Office, various dates.

Webster's American Military Biographies. Springfield, Mass.: Merriam-Webster, 1987.

Progressive Period: The Country

Beale, Howard K. *Theodore Roosevelt and the Rise of America to World Power*. Baltimore: Johns Hopkins Univ. Press, 1956.

Burton, David H. *Theodore Roosevelt, Confident Imperialist*. Philadelphia: Univ. of Pennsylvania Press, 1969.

Chambers, John Whiteclay. *The Tyranny of Change: America in the Progressive Era, 1900–1901*. New York: St. Martin's, 1980.

Faulkner, Harold U. *Politics, Reform and Expansion, 1890–1900*. New York: Harper, 1959.

Fleming, D. F. *The U.S. and the League of Nations, 1918–1920*. New York: Putnam, 1932.

Goldman, Eric F. *Rendezvous with Destiny*. New York: Knopf, 1952.

Hofstader, Richard. *The Age of Reform: From Bryan to FDR*. New York, Knopf, 1955.

Israel, Jerry. *Progressivism and the Open Door: America and China, 1905–1921*. Pittsburgh: Univ. of Pittsburgh Press, 1971.

Link, Arthur. *Woodrow Wilson and the Progressive Era, 1910–1917*. New York: Harper, 1954.

———, and Richard L. McCormick. *Progressivism*. Arlington Heights, Ill.: Harlan Davidson, 1983.

May, Ernest R. *The World War and American Isolation*. Cambridge, Mass.: Harvard Univ. Press, 1959.

May, Henry F. *The End of American Innocence*. New York: Knopf, 1955.

Mowry, George. *The Era of Theodore Roosevelt, 1900–1912*. New York: Harper, 1958.

Pratt, Julius W. *Challenge and Rejection: The United States and World Leadership, 1900–1921*. New York: Macmillan, 1967.

Smith, Arthur H. *China and America Today*. New York: Revell, 1907.

Sullivan, Mark. *Our Times, 1900–1925*. New York: Scribner, 1936.

Progressive Period: The Marines

Bernardo, C. Joseph, and Eugene H. Bacon. *American Military Policy: Its Development since 1775*. Harrisburg, Pa.: Military Service Publishing, 1955.

Catlin, Albertus W. *With the Help of God and a Few Good Marines*. Garden City, N.Y.: Doubleday, 1919.

Challener, Richard D. *Admirals, Generals and American Foreign Policy, 1898–1914*. Princeton, N.J.: Princeton Univ. Press, 1973.

Daniels, Josephus. *The Wilson Era: Years of Peace, 1910–1917*. Chapel Hill: Univ. of North Carolina Press, 1944.

Ellsworth, Captain Harry A. *One Hundred Eighty Landings of the United States Marines, 1800–1934*. Quantico, Va.: Breckinridge Library, MCDEC, 1934.

Grenville, John A. S. *Diplomacy and War Plans in the United States, 1890–1917*. Royal Historical Society, Transactions. 5th Series, no. 2, 1961.

Hammond, Paul. *Organizing for Defense: The American Military Establishment in the Twentieth Century*. Princeton, N.J.: Princeton Univ. Press, 1971.

Heinl, Robert D. *Soldiers of the Sea: The United States Marine Corps, 1775–1962*. Annapolis, Md.: U.S. Naval Institute, 1962.

Hillard, Jack B. *An Annotated Reading List of U.S. Marine Corps History*. Washington, D.C.: U.S. Marine Historical Division, 1971.

U.S. Congress, House Committee on Naval Affairs Hearings, "Status of the Marine Corps," 60th Congress, 2d Session. Washington, D.C.: Government Printing Office, 1909.

Livermore, Seward. "The American Navy as a Factor in World Politics, 1903–1913." *American Historical Review* 63 (1958): 863–79.

Metcalf, Colonel Clyde. *History of the Marine Corps*. New York: Putnam, 1939.

"Report of the Major General Commandant of the USMC." *Annual Reports of the Navy Department*. Washington, D.C.: Government Printing Office.

Shulimson, Jack, and Graham A. Cosmas. "Theodore Roosevelt and the Removal of the Marines from Warships, 1908–1909." Duquesne History Forum, 1979.

Sprout, Harold. *The Rise of American Naval Power, 1776–1918*. Princeton, N.J.: Princeton Univ. Press, 1944.

U.S. Congress, U.S. Department of State. *Foreign Relations of the United States, 1900*. Washington, D.C.: Government Printing Office, 1902.

Varg, Paul. *The Making of a Myth: The U.S. and China, 1897–1912*. East Lansing: Michigan State Univ. Press, 1968.

Vevier, Charles. *The United States and China, 1906–1913*. New York: Greenwood, 1968.

Welch, Richard E., Jr. "American Atrocities in the Philippines: The Indictment and Response." *Pacific Historical Review* 43 (1974): 233–53.

World War I: The Marines, Emerging Chinese Nationalism, Open Doorism, and China Expedition

An Annotated Reading List of USMC History: World War I. Washington, D.C.: History and Museums Division, HQMC, 1967.

Bailey, Thomas. *Woodrow Wilson and the Great Betrayal.* New York: Macmillan, 1945.

Borg, Dorothy. *American Policy and the Chinese Revolution, 1925–1928.* New York: Macmillan, 1947.

Braisted, William R. *The United States Navy in the Pacific, 1909–1922.* Austin: Univ. of Texas Press, 1971.

Buhite, Russell D. *Nelson T. Johnson and American Policy toward China, 1925–41.* East Lansing: Michigan State Univ. Press, 1968.

Buss, Claude Albert. *War and Diplomacy in Eastern Asia.* New York: Macmillan, 1941.

Chiang Kai-shek. *China's Destiny.* New York: Macmillan, 1947.

Dennett, Taylor. *Americans in Eastern Asia: A Critical Study of the Policy of the United States with Reference to China, Japan and Korea in the 19th Century.* New York: Macmillan, 1922.

Fairbank, John. *The United States and China.* Cambridge, Mass.: Harvard Univ. Press, 1948.

Gilbert, Rodney. *What's Wrong with China.* London: John Murray, 1926.

Griswold, Alfred Whitney. *The Far Eastern Policy of the United States.* New York: Harcourt, 1938.

Holcombe, Arthur N. *The Spirit of the Chinese Revolution.* New York: Knopf, 1930.

Hou Chi-ming. *Foreign Investment and Economic Development in China, 1840–1937.* Cambridge, Mass.: Harvard Univ. Press, 1965.

Hull, Cordell. *Memoirs.* 2 vols. New York: Macmillan, 1948.

Iriye, Akira. *After Imperialism: The Search for a New Order in the Far East, 1921–1931.* Cambridge, Mass.: Harvard Univ. Press, 1965.

Johnson, Chalmers. *Peasant Nationalism and Communist Power.* Stanford, Calif.: Stanford Univ. Press, 1962.

Lejeune, John A. *The Reminiscences of a Marine.* Philadelphia: Dorrance, 1930.

May, Ernest R. *The World War and American Isolation, 1914–17.* Cambridge, Mass.: Harvard Univ. Press, 1959.

McClellan, Major E. N. *The United States Marine Corps in the World War.* Washington, D.C.: Historical Division, HQMC, 1920.

Metcalf, Lieutenant Colonel C. H. "The Marines in China." *Marine Corps Gazette* 22 (1938): 35–58.

Morin, Relman. *East Wind Rising.* New York: Knopf, 1960.

Morse, H. B., and H. F. MacNair. *Far Eastern International Relations.* Boston: Houghton-Mifflin, 1931.

Peckham, Charles A. "The Northern Expedition, the Nanking Incident, and the Protection of American Nationals." Master's thesis, Ohio State Univ., 1973.

Pellissier, Roger, ed. *The Awakening of China, 1783–1949.* New York: Putnam, 1967.
Peterson, Horace C. *Propaganda for War: The Campaign against American Neutrality, 1914–17.* Norman: Univ. of Oklahoma Press, 1939.
Reinsch, Paul S. *An American Diplomat in China, 1913–1919.* New York: Doubleday Page, 1922.
Shotwell, James T. *Economic and Social History of the World War.* New Haven, Conn.: Yale Univ. Press, 1924–40.
Stilwell, Joseph W. Personal Papers. Hoover Library, Stanford, California.
Teng, Ssu-yu, and John Fairbank. *China's Response to the West: A Documented Survey, 1839–1923.* Cambridge, Mass.: Harvard Univ. Press, 1954.
Toynbee, Arnold. *A Journey to China.* London: Constable, 1931.
Unpublished Naval Histories in the "Z" File Record Group 45, 1911–27. Washington, D.C.: Naval Historical Division, 1971.
Wilbur, Clarence Martin. *Documents on Communism, Nationalism, and Soviet Advisors in China, 1918–27.* New York: Columbia Univ. Press, 1956.

Indiana: 1905 to the End of World War I

Bailey, Thomas A. *The Man in the Street: The Impact of American Public Opinion on Foreign Policy.* New York: Macmillan, 1948.
Chambers, Frank Pentland. *The War behind the War, 1914–18: A History of the Political and Civilian Fronts.* New York: Harcourt, 1939.
Cummins, Cedric Clisten. "Indiana Public Opinion and the World War, 1914–1917." PhD diss., Indiana Univ., 1976.
Del Vecchio, Richard John. "Indiana Politics during the Progressive Era, 1912–1916." PhD diss., Univ. of Notre Dame, 1973.
Feiney, Frank James. "WWI German-American Sentiment at Saint Meinrad Abbey, Indiana." Master's thesis, Indiana Univ., 1970.
Freeman, Walden S. "Indiana and the League of Nations Issue, 1918–1921, as Reflected in the *Indianapolis News.*" Master's thesis, Butler Univ., 1959.
———. "Will H. Hays and the League of Nations." PhD diss., Indiana Univ., 1967.
Hoy, Suellen Monica. "Samuel Ralston: Progressive Governor, 1913–1917." PhD diss., Indiana Univ., 1975.
Humphreys, Berta Opal. "A Guide to Early Indiana History." Master's thesis, Indiana Univ., 1935.
Phillips, Clifton. *Indiana in Transit, 1880–1920.* Indianapolis: Indiana Historical Society, 1968.
Troyer, Byron. *Yesterday's Indiana.* Miami: Seemann, 1975.
Writer's Program, WPA of Indiana. *Indiana—Guide to the Hoosier State.* New York: Oxford Univ. Press, 1961.

Depression and the New Deal : Shoup and CCC Camps

Allen, Frederick Lewis. *The Lords of Creation*. New York: Harper, 1935.
———. *Since Yesterday: The Nineteen Thirties in America, September 3, 1929–September 3, 1939*. New York: Harper, 1940.
Arndt, H. W. *The Economic Lessons of the Nineteen Thirties*. London: Oxford Univ. Press, 1944.
Beard, Charles, and Mary Beard. *America in Midpassage*. New York: Macmillan, 1939.
Borg, Dorothy. *The United States and the Far Eastern Crisis of 1933–38*. Cambridge, Mass.: Harvard Univ. Press, 1964.
Carr, Edward H. *The Twenty Years' Crisis, 1919–1939: An Introduction to the Study of International Relations*. 2d ed. London: Macmillan, 1946.
Cave, Floyd A. *The Origins and Consequences of World War II*. New York: Dryden, 1948.
Dallek, Robert. *Franklin D. Roosevelt and American Foreign Policy, 1932–1945*. New York: Oxford Univ. Press, 1979.
Ferrell, Robert. *American Diplomacy in the Great Depression*. New Haven, Conn.: Yale Univ. Press, 1957.
Freidel, Frank. *Franklin D. Roosevelt: Launching the New Deal*. Boston: Little, Brown, 1973.
Gunther, John. *Roosevelt in Retrospective*. New York: Harper, 1950.
Rauch, Basil. *The History of the New Deal, 1933–1938*. New York: Creative Age Press, 1944.
Roosevelt, Franklin Delano. *His Personal Letters*. Ed. Elliott Roosevelt. New York: Duell, Sloan, and Pearce, 1950.
Salmond, John. *The Civilian Conservation Corps*. Durham, N.C.: Duke Univ. Press, 1967.
Schlesinger, Arthur M., Jr. *The Crisis of the Old Order*. Boston: Houghton Mifflin, 1957.
Young, Arthur N. *China and the Helping Hand, 1937–1945*. Cambridge, Mass.: Harvard Univ. Press, 1963.

China Revisited: The Shadow of War

Abend, Hallett. *My Life in China, 1926–1941*. New York: Harcourt, 1943.
Alsop, Joseph, "Why We Lost China." *Saturday Evening Post*, 7, 14, and 21, January 1950.
Bland, J. O. P. *China: The Pity of It*. New York: Doubleday, 1932.
Cole, Wayne S. *Roosevelt and the Isolationists, 1932–1945*. Lincoln: Univ. of Nebraska Press, 1983.
Divine, Robert. *The Reluctant Belligerent: American Entry into World War II*. New York: John Wiley, 1965.
Dulles, Foster Rhea. *China and America: The Story of Their Relations since 1784*. Princeton, N.J.: Princeton Univ. Press, 1946.

Epstein, Israel. *The Unfinished Revolution in China*. Boston: Little, Brown, 1947.

Greene, General Wallace M., Jr. Private Papers. Washington, D.C.: Marine Corps Historical Center, Washington Navy Yard.

Gunther, John. *Inside Asia*. New York: Harper, 1939.

Johnson, Chalmers. *Peasant Nationalism and Communist Power: The Emergence of Revolutionary China, 1937–1945*. Stanford, Calif.: Stanford Univ. Press, 1962.

Langer, William L., and Everett Gleason. *The Challenge to Isolation, 1937–40*. New York: Harper, for the Council on Foreign Relations, 1952.

Low, Sir Francis. *The Struggle for Asia*. New York: Praeger, 1956.

Pellissier, Roger, ed. *The Awakening of China, 1738–1949*. New York: Putnam, 1967.

Romanus, Charles F., and Riley Sunderland. *Stilwell's Mission to China*. Washington, D.C.: Office of the Chief of Military History, Department of the Army, 1953.

———. *Time Runs Out in CBI*. Washington, D.C.: Office of the Chief of Military History, Department of Army, 1959.

Snow, Edgar. *Red Star over China*. New York: Random House, 1938.

Stein, Harold. *American Civil-Military Decisions: A Book of Case Studies*. Tuscaloosa: Univ. of Alabama Press, 1963.

Stimson, Henry L., and McGeorge Bundy. *On Active Service in Peace and War*. New York: Harper, 1948.

Tsou Tang. *America's Failure in China, 1941–1950*. Chicago: Univ. of Chicago Press, 1963.

U.S. Department of State. *Far Eastern Series 30—US Relations with China, 1944–1949*. (White Paper.) Washington, D.C.: Government Printing Office, 1949.

World War II Opens

An Annotated Reading List of USMC History: World War II. Washington, D.C.: History and Museums Division, HQMC, 1965.

Asprey, Robert B. *Semper Fidelis*. New York: Norton, 1967.

Brown, Ernest. *The War in Maps: An Atlas of the New York Times Maps*. 4th ed., rev. and enl. New York: Oxford Univ. Press, 1946.

Cave, Floyd A. *The Origins and Consequences of World War II*. New York: Dryden, 1948.

Condit, Kenneth, and Edwin T. Turnbladh. *Hold High the Torch: A History of the 4th Marines*. Washington, D.C.: Historical Branch, HQMC, 1960.

Feis, Herbert. *The China Tangle: The American Effort in China from Pearl Harbor to the Marshall Mission*. Princeton, N.J.: Princeton Univ. Press, 1953.

Guide to the United States Naval Administrative Histories of WWII. Washington, D.C.: Naval Historical Division, 1976.

Johnston, Richard W. *Follow Me: A History of the Second Marine Division in World War II.* New York: Random House, 1948.

Proehl, Captain Carl W. *The 4th Marine Division in World War II.* Washington, D.C.: Infantry Journal Press, 1946.

Shoup, General David M. Personal Papers. Stanford, Calif.: Hoover Institution of War, Peace, and Revolution.

Smith, S. E., ed. *The United States Marines in World War II.* New York: Random House, 1969.

Stembridge, Jasper. *The Oxford War Atlas.* 4 vols. New York: Oxford Univ. Press, 1941–46.

U.S. Department of State. *Foreign Relations of the U.S., 1942, 1943, 1944, China.* 3 vols. Washington, D.C.: Government Printing Office, 1956–68.

U.S. Military Academy, West Point, Department of Military Art and Engineering. *The West Point Atlas of American Wars.* New York: Praeger, 1959.

Watson, Mark S. *Chief of Staff: Prewar Plans and Preparations.* Washington, D.C.: Department of the Army, Historical Division, 1950.

World War II Histories and Historical Reports in the U.S. Naval History Division. Washington, D.C.: Naval Historical Division, 1972.

Pacific War: Tarawa, Tinian, and Saipan

Alexander, Joseph H. *Utmost Savagery: The Three Days of Tarawa.* Annapolis, Md., 1995.

Collier, Basil. *The War in the Far East, 1941–45: A Military History.* New York: Morrow, 1969.

Crowl, Philip Axtell. *Campaign in the Marianas.* Washington, D.C.: Office of the Chief of Military History, Department of the Army, 1960.

———. *Seizure of the Gilberts and Marshalls.* Washington, D.C.: Office of the Chief of Military History, Department of the Army, 1955.

Cunningham, Winfield Scott. *Wake Island Command.* Boston: Little, Brown, 1961.

Devereaux, James Patrick Scott. *The Story of Wake Island.* Philadelphia: Lippincott, 1947.

Hayashi, Saburo, and Alvin D. Coox. *Kogun: The Japanese Army in the Pacific War.* Quantico, Va.: Marine Corps Association, 1959.

Hough, Frank Olney. *The Island War: The United States Marine Corps in the Pacific.* Philadelphia: Lippincott, 1947.

Isely, Jeter A., and Philip A. Crowl. *The U.S. Marines and Amphibious War.* Princeton, N.J.: Princeton Univ. Press, 1951.

King, Ernest Joseph, and Walter Whitehill. *Fleet Admiral King: A Naval Record.* New York: Norton, 1952.

Morton, Louis. *U.S. Army in World War II: The War in the Pacific: Strategy and Command.* Washington, D.C.: Government Printing Office, 1962.

Shaw, Henry I., Jr, Bernard C. Nalty, and Edwin T. Turnbladh. *Central Pacific Drive*. Washington, D.C.: Historical Branch, HQMC, 1966.

Sherrod, Robert Lee. *History of Marine Corps Aviation in World War II.* Washington, D.C.: Combat Forces Press, 1952.

———. *Tarawa: The Story of a Battle*. New York: Duell, Sloan, and Pearce, 1944.

Shoup, General David M. Personal Papers. Stanford, Calif.: Hoover Institution of War, Peace, and Revolution.

Smith, General Holland M., and Percy Finch. *Coral and Brass*. New York: Scribner, 1949.

Toland, John. *The Rising Sun: The Decline and Fall of the Japanese Empire, 1936–45*. New York: Random House, 1970.

Tuchman, Barbara. *Stilwell and the American Experience in China, 1911–1945*. New York: Macmillan, 1971.

Modernizing the Corps, Ribbon Creek, and Fiscal Director

Annual Report of the Commandant to the Secretary of the Navy. Washington, D.C.: USMC Historical Center.

Burgh, Lieutenant General Joseph C. Personal Papers. Washington, D.C.: USMC Historical Center.

Caraley, Demetrios. *The Politics of Military Unification*. New York: Columbia Univ. Press, 1966.

Champie, Elmore A. *A Brief History of the Marine Corps Recruit Depot, Parris Island, S.C., 1891–1962*. Washington, D.C.: Historical Branch, HQMC, 1962.

Fleming, Lieutenant Colonel Charles A. *Quantico: Crossroads of the Marine Corps*. Washington, D.C.: History and Museums Division, HQMC, 1979.

Greene, General Wallace M. Personal Papers. Washington, D.C.: USMC Historical Center.

Hogaboom, General R. E. Personal Papers. Washington, D.C.: USMC Historical Center.

Huntington, Samuel P. *The Soldier and the State*. Cambridge, Mass.: Belknap Press of Harvard Univ. Press, 1957.

Keiser, Gordon W. *The Marine Corps and Defense Unification, 1944–47: The Politics of Survival* (Washington, D.C.: National Defense University Press, 1982).

Kolodziej, Edward A. *The Uncommon Defense and Congress, 1945–1963*. Columbus: Ohio State Univ. Press, 1966.

McKean, W. B. *Ribbon Creek*. New York: Dial, 1958.

Rockefeller Fund. *International Security: The Military Aspect*. New York: Doubleday, 1958.

Shoup, General David M. Personal Papers. Stanford, Calif.: Hoover Institution of War, Peace and Revolution.

Showalter, Dennis. "Evolution of the USMC as a Military Elite." *Marine Corps Gazette,* November 1979.

US Chiefs of Staff. Documents: "JCS 1478-8 through JCS 1478-16." Washington, D.C.: Library of Congress.

USMC. Court of Inquiry records, convened at Parris Island, 9 April 1956. Washington, D.C.: USMC Historical Center.

U.S. Senate, Subcommittee of the Committee on Appropriations. Hearings: Department of Defense Appropriations FY 1955. 83d Congress, 2d session, 1954.

Commandant: New Look to Flex Response

Comptroller General of the U.S. "Overprocurement of Ammunitions by the USMC." Washington, D.C.: Government Printing Office, 1964.

———. "Review of Supply Management Activities, USMC." Washington, D.C.: Government Printing Office, 1960.

Enthoven, Alain C., and K. Wayne Smith. *How Much Is Enough? Shaping the Defense Program, 1961–1969.* New York: Harper, 1971.

Gates, T. S., Acting Secretary of Defense. "Designation, Appointment and Assignment—General Officers." September 24, 1959. Marine Corps File (1959), OF 3-B-17, White House Central Files, Eisenhower Papers.

Halberstam, David. *The Best and the Brightest.* New York: Random House, 1969.

Kinnard, Douglas. *President Eisenhower and Strategy Management.* Lexington: Univ. Press of Kentucky, 1977.

Korb, Lawrence. *The Joint Chiefs of Staff.* Bloomington: Indiana Univ. Press, 1976.

McCutcheon, General Keith B. Personal Papers. Washington, D.C.: USMC Historical Center.

Schilling, Warner R., Paul Hammond, and Glenn Snyder. New York: Columbia Univ. Press, 1962.

Snyder, Glenn H. "The 'New Look' of 1953." In *Strategy, Policy and Defense Budgets,* ed.

Sorenson, Theodore. *Kennedy.* New York: Harper, 1965.

Stapleton, Margaret. *The Truman and Eisenhower Years: A Selective Bibliography.* Metuchen, N.J.: Scarecrow Press, 1973.

U.S. House of Representatives, Committee on Armed Forces Hearings: "Military Posture and Appropriations FY 1964." 88th Congress, 1st Session, 1963.

Vietnam War Protester

Benis, Frank M. *Marine Corps Operations in Vietnam: Field Interviews.* Washington, D.C.: History and Museums Division, HQMC, 1975.

Buttinger, Joseph. *Vietnam: A Dragon Embattled*. New York: Praeger, 1967.

Chaisson, Lieutenant General John R. Correspondence. Stanford, Calif.: Hoover Institution of War, Peace, and Revolution.

Cooper, Chester L. *The Lost Crusade: America in Vietnam*. New York: Dodd, Mead, 1970.

Corson, Lieutenant Colonel William R., USMC (Ret.). *The Betrayal*. New York: Norton, 1968.

Fall, Bernard B. *The Two Vietnams*. Rev. ed. New York: Praeger, 1964.

Giap, Vo Nguyen. *Peoples' War, Peoples' Army*. Hanoi: Foreign Language Publishing House, 1961.

Krulak, Lt. General V. H. "A Strategic Appraisal, Vietnam, December 1965." Washington, D.C.: USMC Historical Center.

———. Personal Papers. Washington, D.C.: USMC Historical Division.

Leckie, Robert. *The March to Glory*. New York: World, 1960.

Lewy, Gunther. *America in Vietnam*. New York: Oxford Univ. Press, 1978.

Lindsay, Robert. *This High Name: Public Relations and the USMC*. Madison: Univ. of Wisconsin Press, 1956.

Montgomery, John D. *The Politics of Foreign Aid: American Experience in Southeast Asia*. New York: Praeger, 1962.

Shulimson, Jack. *U.S. Marines in Vietnam: An Expanding War, 1966*. Washington, D.C.: History and Museums Division, HQMC, 1978.

Simmons, Brigadier General Edwin H. *The Marines in Vietnam, 1954–73: An Anthology and Annotated Bibliography*. Washington, D.C.: History and Museums Division, HQMC, 1974.

Thompson, Sir Robert. *No Exit from Vietnam*. New York: McKay, 1969.

U.S. Pacific Command. "Report on the War in Vietnam as of 30 June 1968." Washington, D.C.: Government Printing Office, 1969.

Walt, General Lewis W. *Strange War, Strange Strategy*. New York: Funk and Wagnalls, 1970.

Whitlow, Captain Robert H. *U.S. Marines in Vietnam, 1954–64*. Washington, D.C.: History and Museums Division, HQMC, 1977.

Miscellaneous

Biderman, Albert D. "Where Do They Go from Here?—Retired Military in America. *Annals of the American Academy of Political and Social Sciences*, 406 (1973): 146–61.

Index

About the Author

Howard Jablon is professor of history at Purdue University, North Central. His main interests include the history of American diplomacy during the New Deal period and national security policy during the Vietnam War. He is author of numerous articles and a book on the State Department in the Franklin D. Roosevelt era, *Crossroads of Decision*. He and his wife live in Michiana Shores, Indiana.